SO-BJM-696

# THE APPROVED
# BOATING
## HANDBOOK: Boat Pro

 Transport Transports
Canada Canada

This course meets the minimum requirements of basic boating safety knowledge as set out in the Transport Canada Boating Safety Course guidelines. This course has also been approved by the U.S. National Association of State Boating Law Administrators.

All references to specific laws contained in this publication have been compiled from sources believed to be the most recent and reliable, and to represent the best current opinion on the subject. No warranty, guarantee, or representation is made by Canadian Power & Sail Squadrons as to the absolute legal correctness or sufficiency of any representation contained in this publication.

# The Approved Boating Handbook: Boat Pro

Published by Canadian Power & Sail Squadrons
Escadrilles canadiennes de plaisance
Toronto, Ontario
1st Edition © Canadian Power & Sail Squadrons 2007 (revised 2009)

Distributed by Map Art Corporation, a company owned by Peter Heiler Ltd, through its
distribution network.

All rights reserved. No part of this publication may be reproduced, stored in a retrieval
system, or transmitted in any form, or by any means—electronic, mechanical photocopying,
recording, or otherwise—without the written permission of Canadian Power & Sail
Squadrons.

**Canadian Power & Sail Squadrons**
26 Golden Gate Court
Toronto, Ontario M1P 3A5 Canada
Phone:  416-293-2438 or 1-888-CPS-BOAT
Internet: www.cps-ecp.ca
Printed in Canada

ISBN: 978-1-55368-600-2

**PHOTOS USED BY PERMISSION OF:**
Les Armstrong: page 34 (right)
Gary Scott Breithaupt: pages 13, 34 (left), 35 (left), 43, 49, 57 (right)
BRP US Inc.: page 4 (left)
Canadian Marine Manufacturers Association: page 56 (left)
Environment Canada: page 105
Lowe Boats: page 1 (left), 2 (left)
Mercury Marine: pages 4 (right), 5 (left)
Mustang Survival Corp.: cover (middle, right), pages 5 (middle), 18, 69
Ontario Federation of Anglers & Hunters: page 64 (left)
Salus Marine Wear: page 16 (middle)
Vanessa Schmidt: pages, 8 22 (top, middle), 36, 38, 39, 50 (right), 61–63,
64 (right), 70, 71 (left), 83, 91, 92, 101, 103
Simrad Inc.: page 79
U.S. Coast Guard: cover (left, right top and bottom), pages 6 (left), 17 (left),
32 (left), 35 (right), 77, 95–98
Yamaha Motor Canada Ltd.: pages 67, 71 (right), 87

# Transport Canada regulations

Effective April 1, 1999, the Canadian Coast Guard Office of Boating Safety (now Transport Canada Office of Boating Safety) introduced new regulations for operators of pleasure boats fitted with a motor and used for recreational purposes.

Also effective April 1, 1999*– if you are under 12 years of age, and not directly supervised**, you are not to operate a power-driven boat of more than 10 hp. If you are over 12, but under 16, and not directly supervised**, you are not to operate a power-driven boat of more than 40 hp.

| Dates of requisition of competency proof on board | |
| --- | --- |
| Since September 15, 1999 | All operators born after April 1, 1983 must carry proof of competency at all times. |
| Since September 15, 2002 | All operators of craft less than 4 m (13'1") in length, including personal watercraft must carry proof of competency at all times. |
| **September 15, 2009** | **All operators of any powered craft must carry proof of competency at all times.** |

Applies to non-residents operating their pleasure craft in Canadian waters after 45 consecutive days. Operator card or equivalent issued to a non-resident by their state or country will be considered as proof of competency.

\* These requirements apply in areas outside the Northwest Territories and Nunavut at this time.

\*\* Directly supervised means accompanied and directly supervised in the boat by a person 16 years of age or older.

## Introduction

Boating can be fun and safe for the whole family. With basic knowledge and care a boater can avoid trouble instead of trying to get out of it. When operating a boat you are responsible for:
- the safety of the boat
- the safety of your guests
- any damage caused by your boat or its wake

Boaters must keep up to date on changes in boating regulations that may affect:
- the equipment they require
- where and how they can operate their boat
- boating safety in general

Prudent operators will continue their boating knowledge by taking additional courses in boating safety and navigation.

The Criminal Code of Canada prohibits a person from operating a boat that is not seaworthy and operating a boat in a manner that is dangerous to the public.

Every year several thousand boating incidents are reported to the various enforcement authorities. The most frequently reported incidents are mechanical failures (or lack of fuel). The most frequent types of non-fatal accidents are collisions with other boats or with fixed objects. The most common fatal accidents involve capsizing and falling overboard. Fires and explosions, though less common, cause the highest percentage of property losses.

In Canada, all boaters are governed by the following acts, codes and regulations. Those who contravene them are subject to penalties or fines. This manual is designed to make you familiar with the applicable portions of these regulations.

1. Canada Shipping Act (CSA)
2. Contraventions Act
3. Boating Restriction Regulations
4. Charts and Nautical Publications Regulations
5. Collision Regulations
6. Small Vessel Regulations, and
7. Criminal Code of Canada

Regardless of the type of boat you have, all safety equipment must be:
- in good operating order,
- easily accessible,
- approved by Transport Canada (TC) and/or Fisheries and Oceans.

This manual is an introduction to the legal, and safe, practices of boating. It applies to all those who use a boat. This manual is suitable either as a home-study course or for in-class instruction of approximately eight hours. The accredited Examination must be written under supervised conditions. A valuable additional reference is the Safe Boating Guide, published by the Transport Canada, free at marinas and nautical bookstores, or order a free copy online at http://shop.tc.gc.ca.

# Home study

Upon completion of the home-study manual, if you wish to obtain the Transport Canada's (TC) Pleasure Craft Operator Card, you will need to make arrangements to write a supervised examination. (There is an examination fee.) Please call the CPS office and we can make the necessary arrangements. Successfully complete the examination and a TC Pleasure Craft Operator Card will be forwarded to you.

Upon successful completion of the Boat Pro examination, CPS will be pleased to offer you a complimentary Associate Membership* to join our organization. After the first year, there is an annual fee which is usually offset by the many benefits available to you. Additional information on this special offer will be provided when you receive your TC Pleasure Craft Operator Card.

This course is also available on-line through our Open Learning Centre. Explore our Web site at www.cps-ecp.ca, and enhance your learning experience.

If you should have any questions, please call or E-mail us at the numbers noted below.

**Telephone:** (416) 293-2438 or 1-888-CPS-BOAT

**E-mail:** hqg@cps-ecp.ca

**Web site:** www.cps-ecp.ca

Thank you, and safe boating!

> The Pleasure Craft Operator Card shows you have rudimentary boating information. After you have boated for a while and find you need more nautical knowledge the CPS BOATING COURSE is a good next step.

## About Canadian Power & Sail Squadrons

Canadian Power & Sail Squadrons (CPS) is a nationwide organization of recreational boating enthusiasts. CPS is a charitable organization with 30,000 active members. Our volunteer instructors help recreational boaters improve their boating safety knowledge as well as their vessel handling and navigation skills. Students successfully completing the Boating course or this course will receive a one year complimentary membership*.

Membership in Canadian Power & Sail Squadrons means that you are part of a community of passionate boaters who are committed to safety, boating education and having fun on the water! CPS has been connecting enthusiastic boaters for years and has played a major role in boating culture in Canada. Members have access to a huge network of new friends, educators and enthusiasts, all of whom recognize that CPS is the established leader and trend setter for recreational boating in this country. In addition to the social benefits of CPS members also receive discounts on boat, home, auto insurance and nautical equipment. For our complete list of benefits visit: www.cps-ecp.ca.

## You are in good company!

A respected and influential advocate for boaters, CPS works closely with many other organizations to voice concerns and recommendations:

- Canadian Yachting Association
- Provincial Marine Operators Associations
- Canadian Marine Manufacturers Association
- Canadian Safe Boating Council
- Regional and National Recreational Boating Advisory Councils

We also work closely with Transport Canada, Industry Canada, Fisheries and Oceans and the Canadian Coast Guard Auxiliary. As a member of CPS, you are supporting the creation and maintenance of a safe, beautiful and enjoyable boating environment for all Canadians!

*This offer is valid at time of printing and may be discontinued.

# Table of Contents

# Know your boat

## Boating terminology

Many of the terms used in boating are not common in everyday speech. These specialized words can save time. They can tell in one or two words ideas that might take many words to express. For example, boaters would not refer to another boat as being "straight out from the middle of the left side of our boat, and at right angles to our centre line". They would describe the other boat as being "abeam to port". A small glossary of boating terms is at the back of the manual.

Memory aid: Port and left have four letters. Or with my right finger I point to the starboard.

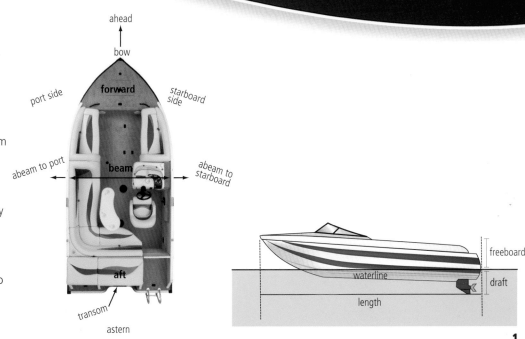

## Types of boat

There are many types of boat, each made for a particular use. A boat designed for one use may not be suitable for a different one. For example, a bass fishing boat is not safe on the ocean. A boat with a deep "V" hull will have problems in a shallow lake.

When you buy a boat, you need to keep in mind the type of boating you want to do. Never choose a boat only because of its price. If you are to use it safely, and to enjoy it for many years, it must be sturdy and designed for your use. Choose a boat which can safely carry the equipment you need and the required safety items.

Remember, a personal watercraft (PWC) is a boat. It must obey all the boating rules and regulations.

Boat hulls are of two basic designs: **Planing** and **Displacement.** All hulls sit in the water when they are stationary or when moving slowly.

When you increase the speed on a planing boat it begins to rise up on its bow wave. As it accelerates it climbs over its bow wave and skims along the water's surface. Planing boats can travel at high speed. Unless the water surface is flat, or nearly so, they tend to pound with the waves. A displacement boat moves through the water and pushes it aside. This movement creates a bow wave. Regardless of speed,

a displacement boat will not climb over this bow wave. Displacement boats ride comfortably, even in rough seas, but cannot go very fast.

As boats, both planing and displacement, start to climb up on their bow wave they can make a very large wake. It is this large wake that can cause damage to others. It is at these times that power boaters must be aware of who and what is around them.

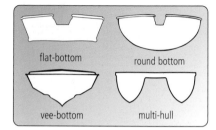

flat-bottom     round bottom

vee-bottom     multi-hull

**Flat-bottom Boat:** These are inexpensive to build, have a shallow draft, and plane easily. They are good for shallow water, utility and racing boats but in rough water can be quite tippy and tend to pound.

**Round-bottom Boat:** These move easily through the water, but tend to be less stable. Examples are canoes and some sailboats. These boats have a tendency to roll, unless they have a deep keel or stabilizers.

**Vee-bottom Boat:** These give a smoother ride in choppy water, and are often used

as runabouts. The Deep-V is a further improvement, with a sharper entry into the water.

**Multi-hull Boat:** Catamarans have two hulls and trimarans have three hulls. This design provides great stability and is often used in sailboats and houseboats.

## Powering your boat

Boats such as rowboats and canoes are usually powered using oars or paddles. However, most boats have engines or use wind power. The most common fuel used is gasoline. Four different types of power unit are discussed below.

Selecting the proper engine to power your boat is very important. Choosing too small an engine will cause it to work very hard all the time and will reduce performance. Too large an engine can overpower the boat. Using a larger

engine that a boat wasn't designed to handle can damage the boat and hurt passengers.

> ⚠️ When a sailboat uses its engine, it is legally a power boat. This is true even if it is using its sails at the same time the engine is running. As a power boat, it is subject to "power boat" Regulations. When motoring, it loses any privileges due to boats which are under sail only.

## Outboard

These are the most popular drives on small boats. They are powerful for their size and are very adaptable. An outboard producing 7.5 kW can be carried easily. It can be clamped in a matter of minutes to the transom (the flat part of the stern). Power is transmitted to a propeller. As the outboard swivels, it steers the boat. Many outboards are two cycle. These engines require oil to be mixed with the fuel to lubricate the engine. There are many kinds of oil and mixture requirements.

Check in the owners' manual or with the dealer.

In recent years, an increasing number of four-stroke-cycle engines have come on the market. The oil is held in a sump or crankcase. Exhaust is more environmentally friendly, engines tend to be quieter, have fewer vibrations and be more fuel efficient. These engines may be heavier and can adversely affect the balance of the boat

In addition to the traditional outboard there are many models of electric trolling motors.

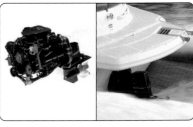

## Stern drive

These are also referred to as I/Os, (Inboard/Outboard). The drive and engine are usually heavier than outboards. Stern drives produce more power, usually use gasoline as a fuel, and are four-stroke-cycle engines. They are mounted inside the hull. Their power is transmitted to a propeller through a stern drive, which is mounted through the transom. For steering the stern drive can swivel from side to side like an outboard engine. It can also be tilted, up or down.

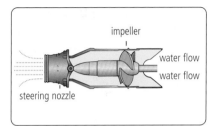

## Inboard

These are usually four-stroke-cycle gasoline or diesel engines that are mounted inside the hull. Power is transmitted to a propeller by a shaft through the bottom of the boat. The propeller shaft is supported outside the hull by a strut. The shaft cannot be moved from side to side. A rudder is mounted close behind the propeller. The boat is steered using the discharge current from the propeller.

## Personal watercraft (PWC)/jet boat

The engine of a jet boat is also mounted inboard. Instead of having a propeller, the engine drives a pump that sucks water through an intake and discharges it out the back. The water leaves at high pressure through a nozzle. There is no rudder. The boat is steered by moving the nozzle left or right. For steering control, power must be maintained to the pump. If a jet boat is at idle or if the accelerator has been released, the boat cannot be steered.

It goes straight ahead. **For steering control, power must be maintained to the pump.**

The other feature of the jet propulsion system is that the operator may fall overboard and reboard the craft, without risk of propeller injury.

> ⚠ Boats equipped with exhaust pipes ejecting directly into the air are not permitted to operate within five miles of shore. When operating within five miles of shore, noise abatement mechanism, mufflers, must be in use at all times.

Capacity plates

Conformity and Single Vessel labels

## Paddle sports

These days, paddlers are everywhere. Power boaters must pay close attention when boating near paddlers or any small boat. Give them wide berth and slow right down, 8 – 10 k.p.h. **Leave no wake.** Recognize that they may have limited ability to manoeuvre and limited stability. Make sure they are aware of your intentions and be courteous.

## Canadian compliance plates

Note: Plates or labels issued in another country or by anyone other than the Canadian Government are not valid for Canadian registered or licensed boats.

All new pleasure boats sold in Canada up to 6m in length and capable of being fitted with an engine(s) of 7.5¹ kW or more are required to carry a Capacity Plate. These plates must be permanently attached, and in plain view. Requirements for Capacity Plates changed from 5 to 6m on April 1, 1999. Plates issued before that date are still valid. Existing pleasure

craft that do not have a Compliance Notice do not need to obtain one. A pleasure craft owner is not expected to obtain a Compliance Notice if the manufacturer failed to attach one. Currently it is an offense to operate a pleasure craft that does not have a Compliance Notice. This offense will be removed from the regulations.

The capacity plate states the safe limits for the vessel of:
- engine power which is the recommended outboard engine size,
- the number of persons onboard, and

| Length of Boat | Number of Persons | Maximum Load* |
|---|---|---|
| 3m | 2 | 185 kg |
| 3.7m | 3 | 260 kg |
| 4m | 4 | 335 kg |
| not over 6m | 5 | 440 kg |

* Including weight of people, engine, fuel, equipment, etc. In rough water, there should be at least one less person in the boat.

- the maximum total load in kilograms which includes persons, equipment, stores, engine, and fuel.

It also confirms that the vessel is built to Canadian Government Construction Standards.

All other motorized pleasure craft sold in Canada are required to display a Conformity Plate or label. This plate states that the vessel meets the Construction Standards that are issued by the Canadian Coast Guard or Transport Canada.

The Single Vessel label is issued to home built boats or those boats built by a builder who is no longer able to supply a label. The Single Vessel label programme is being phased out.

The load that can be safely carried in a boat depends on:
- the type of boat
- the amount of equipment
- the number of passengers
- the weight distribution

The Canadian Coast Guard recommends the above weight loads based on the length of the boat. These are only a guide. All operators should be aware of any other limitations of their boat.

## Boat licensing

Understand that personal watercraft are classified as boats. All boats under 15 tons gross and powered by an engine of 7.5kW[1] or more must be licensed. Licenses can be obtained, free of charge, from any Service Canada office. The Small Vessel Regulations state that a license number must be displayed in block characters, in a contrasting colour and with characters no less than 7.5 cm high on each side of the bow. Boats with smaller engines can also be licensed if the owner wishes. In

[1] 7.5kW is about 10 horsepower.

addition to attaching the license number to the boat the owner must carry the paper certificate on board. Placing it in a watertight envelope is recommended.

New vessel licenses, transfers and renewals will be valid for 10 years. Existing licenses without an expiry date are grandfathered unless the information on the license has changed since it was issued. License holders must report a change in name or address and obtain a renewed license within 30 days of the change.

Provincially licensed amphibious vessels will no longer be exempt from these regulations.

## Boat registration

Pleasure craft of 15 or more tons gross must be registered with the Registrar of Shipping. However, smaller boats may also be "registered". To register, the vessel must be measured by a surveyor of ships from the Ship Safety Branch of Transport Canada. A registration fee will be charged. Every boat so registered must be permanently marked with a unique name on the bow and the name of Port of Registry on the stern. An official number and the registered tonnage of the vessel are to be permanently marked on the inside of the hull, in a conspicuous place and in such a way so as to make removal impossible.

## US boat identification

If you plan to purchase a boat in the US, or import one, you should be aware of two additional items. A Hull Identification Number (HIN) is like the serial number on a car. All US recreational boats built after October, 1972, must have one. The number consists of 12 characters, no less than one-fourth of an inch high. The HIN appears in two places. If the boat has a transom, one of the numbers will be on the starboard side within two inches of its top. If it doesn't have a transom, the number will be on the top of the hull within two feet of the stern. On pontoon boats, it is on the AFT crossbeam within one foot of the starboard hull attachment. The boat also has a duplicate number in an unexposed location. It is on the interior or under a fitting or hardware item. The Capacity Plate for boats made in the US

**8**

complies with US Coast Guard Safety Standards.

## Security requirements when visiting US waters

In the wake of the events of September 11, 2001, United States authorities have established a number of new homeland security requirements. Anyone operating a boat in US waters must abide by these requirements.

### US naval vessel protection zone

Vessels are prohibited from passing within 100 yards (92 metres) of any US naval vessel. If it is essential for a vessel to enter this zone that vessel must first contact the US naval vessel or its US Coast Guard escort vessel or the official patrol. Contact can be made using a VHF radio on Channel 16. The vessel may then proceed only as directed.

Between 500 yards (458 metres) and 100 yards, vessels approaching a US naval vessel are required to operate at the minimum speed necessary to maintain a safe course. In this area they are to proceed as directed by the commanding officer of the US naval vessel in question or the official patrol.

Any vessel failing to abide by these requirements will be subject to immediate boarding by US authorities. The violators face a prison term of up to six years and a fine of up to 250,000 US dollars.

Approaching certain other commercial vessels may result in immediate boarding by US authorities.

## Other US security zones

There are several other kinds of security zones of which boaters visiting the US must be aware. Listed below are specific security warnings transcribed from US Coast Guard publications:

- "Observe and avoid all security zones. Avoid commercial port operation areas, especially those that involve military, cruise-line, or petroleum facilities. Observe and avoid other restricted areas near dams, power plants. Violators will be perceived as a threat, and will face a quick, determined, and severe response."
- "Do not stop or anchor beneath bridges or in the channel. If you do, then expect to be boarded by law enforcement officials."
- "Keep a sharp eye out for anything that looks peculiar or out of the ordinary. Report all activities that seem suspicious to the local authorities, the Coast Guard or the port or marina security. Do not

approach or challenge those acting in a suspicious manner."

## Using current information

Anyone intending to operate a boat in US waters should, before leaving Canada, obtain the latest update of the US homeland security requirements set out above. They should also obtain full information regarding other matters such as: US immigration and customs requirements, US boat licensing requirements and US maritime VHF radio licensing requirements.

The US Coast Guard, US Immigration and Customs Enforcement are part of the US Department of Homeland Security. Its website is <http://www.dhs.gov/>.

## SECTION 1: Know your boat

From the four possible answers given below, select the one you think is most nearly correct.

1. **When you buy a boat, you should think primarily of:**
   A. the cost
   B. the kind of boating you want to do
   C. the boat's appearance
   D. the name of the manufacturer

2. **A displacement vessel:**
   A. goes faster every time a larger engine is fitted
   B. pushes its way through the water
   C. usually has a flat bottom
   D. must have a mast

3. **Boats must be licensed, if they:**
   A. have an engine that is less than 4 kW (5 hp)
   B. have an engine that is more than 4 kW (5 hp)
   C. have an engine that is 7.5 kW (10 hp) or more
   D. have any engine at all

4. **If something is "abeam to port", it is:**
   A. straight out sideways from the middle of the boat, on the left side
   B. straight out sideways from the middle of the boat, on the right side
   C. behind you and to the right
   D. in front of you, to the left

5. **Planing hulls:**
   A. are usually found on large-keel boats
   B. cannot go very fast
   C. are designed to skim over the water
   D. have deep vee bottoms

6. **Most small utility boats:**
   A. are made of wood
   B. are flat-bottom
   C. are comfortable in rough water
   D. cannot be power driven

7.  **If a small boat is underpowered:**
    **A.** The boat becomes unmanageable.
    **B.** The insurance rate will be reduced.
    **C.** The engine will work too hard, and performance will suffer.
    **D.** Gas consumption improves dramatically.

8.  **The license numbers on a boat must be in letters that are:**
    **A.** 7.5 cms high
    **B.** written in fancy script
    **C.** almost the same colour as the boat, so as not to be conspicuous
    **D.** displayed at the stern

9.  **Which of the following is a displacement vessel?**
    **A.** a deep-keeled sailboat
    **B.** a personal watercraft
    **C.** a runabout
    **D.** an open fishing boat

10. **A capacity plate gives:**
    **A.** the boat's speed
    **B.** the weight of the boat when empty
    **C.** gross load capacity and recommended engine size
    **D.** the number of life jackets that must be carried

11. **If the engine on a PWC stops unexpectedly:**
    **A.** the boat loses buoyancy and may sink
    **B.** the boat cannot be steered
    **C.** the engine cannot be restarted at sea
    **D.** the boat becomes unstable and may capsize

| Answers | | |
|---|---|---|
| 1-b | 4-a | 8-a |
| 2-b | 5-c | 9-a |
| 3-c | 6-b | 10-c |
| | 7-c | 11-b |

# Equipping your boat

## Required equipment

All boats are required to carry certain
equipment. Some items must be approved
by Transport Canada. All items must be in
good working order, must be maintained
in accordance with the manufacturer's
instructions and must be immediately
available in case of emergency.

| | Sailboards | Paddleboats & watercycles | Canoes, kayaks, rowboats & rowing shells | Unpowered pleasure craft | Personal watercraft (PWC) |
|---|---|---|---|---|---|
| **Personal protection equipment** | -One Canadian-approved PFD or life jacket of appropriate size for each person on board<br><br>-One buoyant heaving line no less than 15 m in length | -One Canadian-approved PFD or life jacket of appropriate size for each person on board<br><br>-One buoyant heaving line no less than 15 m in length (exempt if all people on board wear a PFD) | -One Canadian-approved PFD or life jacket of appropriate size for each person on board<br><br>-One buoyant heaving line no less than 15 m in length | -One Canadian-approved PFD or life jacket of appropriate size for each person on board<br><br>-One buoyant heaving line no less than 15 m in length | -One Canadian-approved personal flotation device or life jacket of appropriate size for each person on board<br><br>-One buoyant heaving line no less than 15 m in length |
| **Boat safety equipment** | -One manual propelling device | -Not required | -One manual propelling device or an anchor with 15 m line<br><br>-Bailer or manual water pump | -Manual propelling device or an anchor with 15 m line<br><br>-One Class 5BC fire extinguisher (if equipped with a fuel-burning cooking, heating or refrigerating appliance)<br><br>-Bailer or manual water pump fitted with sufficient hose to enable a person using the pump to discharge water from the bilge of the vessel over the side of the vessel * | -One manual propelling device or an anchor with 15 m line length  (exempt if all people on board wear a PFD)<br>-Bailer or manual water pump fitted with sufficient hose to enable a person using the pump to discharge water from the bilge of the vessel over the side of the vessel length (exempt if all people on board wear a PFD)<br>-One Class 5BC fire extinguisher length (exempt if all people on board wear a PFD) |
| **Distress equipment** | -A watertight flashlight or Three (3) Canadian-approved flares of Type A, B or C (exempt if all people on board wear a PFD) | -A watertight flashlight or Three (3) Canadian-approved flares of Type A, B or C (exempt if all people on board wear a PFD) | -Not required | -Not required | -A watertight flashlight **or** Three (3) Canadian-approved flares of Type A, B or C |
| **Navigation equipment** | -A sound-signalling device | -A sound-signalling device,<br>-Navigation lights or watertight flashlight if operated at night or during periods of poor visibility. | -A sound-signalling device,<br>-Navigation lights or watertight flashlight  if operated at night or during periods of poor visibility | -A sound-signalling device,<br>-Navigation lights or watertight flashlight  if operated at night or during periods of poor visibility. | A sound-signalling device |

Note: A bailer or pump is not required for any self-bailing sealed hull sailing vessel fitted with a recess-type cockpit that cannot contain enough water to make the vessel capsize or a multi-hull vessel that has subdivided multiple sealed hull construction. For

| | Up to 6 m powered | Over 6 m but not over 9 m | Over 9 m but not over 12 m | 12 m but not over 24 m | Over 24 m |
|---|---|---|---|---|---|
| **Personal protection equipment** | -PFD or life jacket of appropriate size for each person on board<br>-15 m buoyant heaving line | -PFD or life jacket of appropriate size for each person on board<br>-15 m buoyant heaving line or lifebuoy with 15 m of buoyant line attached<br>-Reboarding device if the height that must be climbed from the water is greater than 0.5 m | -PFD or life jacket of appropriate size for each person on board<br>-15 m buoyant heaving line and -lifebuoy with 15 m of buoyant line attached<br>-Reboarding device if the height that must be climbed from the water is greater than 0.5 m | -PFD or life jacket of appropriate size for each person on board<br>-15 m buoyant heaving line<br>-lifebuoy equipped with a self-igniting light and 15 m of buoyant line attached<br>-Reboarding device if the height that must be climbed from the water is greater than 0.5 m | -PFD or life jacket of appropriate size for each person on board<br>-30 m of buoyant heaving line. Two lifebuoys with 30 m of buoyant line attached with self-igniting light<br>-Reboarding device if the height that must be climbed from the water is greater than 0.5 m plus a lifting harness & rigging |
| **Boat safety equipment** | -One manual propelling device or an anchor with no less than 15 m of line<br>-Bailer or manual water pump fitted with sufficient hose to enable a person using the pump to discharge water from the bilge of the vessel over the side of the vessel<br>-One Class 5BC fire extinguisher, if the pleasure craft is equipped with an inboard engine, a fixed fuel tank of any size, or a fuel-burning cooking, heating or refrigerating appliance | -One manual propelling device or an anchor with no less than 15 m of line<br>-Bailer or a manual water pump fitted with sufficient hose to enable a person using the pump to discharge water from the bilge of the vessel over the side of the vessel<br>-One Class 5BC fire extinguisher if power-driven plus one Class 5BC fire extinguisher if equipped with a fuel burning appliance | -An anchor with no less than 30 m of line<br>-Bailer<br>-Manual water pump fitted with sufficient hose to enable a person using the pump to discharge water from the bilge of the vessel over the side of the vessel<br>-One Class 10BC fire extinguisher and one Class 10BC fire extinguisher if equipped with a fuel burning appliance | -An anchor with no less than 50 m of line<br>-Bilge pumping arrangements<br>-One Class 10BC fire extinguisher at each of the following:<br>-entrance to any space where fuel burning appliance is present<br>-entrance to any accommodation space<br>-entrance to engine room<br>-Axe<br>-2 buckets, each with a capacity of 10 L or more | -An anchor with no less than 50 m of line<br>-Bilge pumping arrangements<br>-One Class 10BC fire extinguisher at each of the following:<br>-entrance to any space where fuel burning appliance is present<br>-entrance to any accommodation space<br>-entrance to engine room<br>-Axe<br>-4 buckets, each with a capacity of 10 L or more |
| **Distress equipment** | -A watertight flashlight or<br>-3 Canadian-approved flares of Type A, B or C | -A watertight flashlight<br>-6 Canadian-approved flares of Type A, B or C | -A watertight flashlight<br>-12 Canadian-approved flares of Type A, B, C or D, no more than six of which are of Type D | -A watertight flashlight<br>-12 Canadian-approved flares of Type A, B, C or D, no more than six of which are of Type D | -A watertight flashlight<br>-12 Canadian-approved flares of Type A, B, C or D, no more than six of which are of Type D |
| **Navigation equipment** | -A sound-signalling device or a sound-signalling appliance<br>-Navigation lights (if operated at night or during periods of poor visibility)<br>-magnetic compass* | -A sound-signalling device or a sound-signalling appliance<br>-Navigation lights (if operated at night or during periods of poor visibility)<br>-magnetic compass* | -A sound-signalling device or a sound-signalling appliance<br>-Navigation lights (as per the *Canadian Collision Regulations*)<br>-magnetic compass | -A sound-signalling device or a sound-signalling appliance<br>-Navigation lights (as per the *Canadian Collision Regulations*)<br>-magnetic compass | -A sound-signalling device or a sound-signalling appliance<br>-Navigation lights (as per the *Canadian Collision Regulations*)<br>-magnetic compass |

*Not required if the vessel is operated within sight of navigation marks.

## Personal Flotation Device (PFD)

- For a PWC rider
- a white water paddler
- a person less than 16 years of age or a person weighing less than 36.3 kg, the PFD must be an inherently buoyant type, not an inflatable

In all other cases, a PFD may be of the inflatable type in any open boat, if worn. If the boat is not open the PFD may be of the inflatable type if worn while on deck or in the cockpit or is readily available to a person who is below deck.

A PFD or lifejacket is not required to fit an infant weighing less than 9 kg or any person whose chest size exceeds 140 cm but there must be a PFD or lifejacket on board for those persons.

PFDs do not work unless they are being worn. In 2001 over 80 % of boating related drowning victims were not wearing PFDs. A boat operator must be aware of changing conditions. An operator should inform each person on board that they should be wearing a PFD:

- in severe weather
- in dangerous water conditions
- in areas of high boat traffic
- around dangerous local hazards
- when away from shore or operating at night

It is difficult to put on a PFD or lifejacket once you are in the water. It only takes one try to convince anyone of this fact.

Note: In the United States there are a number of State and Federal regulations that require PFD wear by certain children aboard recreational vessels.

## Your life jacket or PFD

It should be of appropriate size, snug-fitting, yet allow freedom of movement of arms and legs. A PFD must not be used to sit on, kneel on or as padding to protect your boat from the dock.

Check each PFD's buoyancy regularly. Wade out until the water is chest-deep. Bend your knees and see that you float with your chin above water so that it is easy to breathe. You should allow your flotation device to dry in the open air. Do not constantly expose a PFD to sunlight or dry it close to a direct heat source.

PFD's should be kept readily accessible in a dry, well-ventilated area. The approved status of a flotation device is void if it has been repaired or altered.

**A PFD should:**
- be cleaned with mild soap and water
- not be dry cleaned or washed using strong detergents
- never be cleaned with gasoline.

Operators of pleasure craft should always wear their lifejackets, or PFDs, to prevent drowning. They should learn how to put them on in the water.

**Practise the following steps in the water:**
1. Spread the device open with the inside facing up out of the water.
2. Rotate the device so as to look at the neck opening.
3. Extend both arms through arm openings.
4. Lift arms over the head.
5. Position the device around the upper body
6. Fasten the device to fit snugly.

Compared to an adult, a child's body weight is distributed differently. They do not float well in a face-up position, and tend to panic easily. Ensure that the PFD or life jacket is "child-sized." Remember that a life jacket or PFD is no substitute for adult supervision.

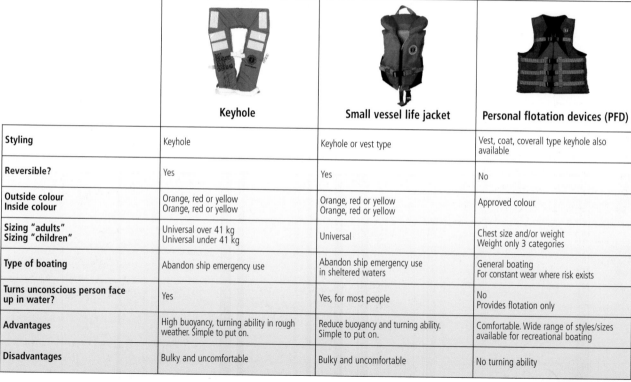

| | Keyhole | Small vessel life jacket | Personal flotation devices (PFD) |
|---|---|---|---|
| **Styling** | Keyhole | Keyhole or vest type | Vest, coat, coverall type keyhole also available |
| **Reversible?** | Yes | Yes | No |
| **Outside colour**<br>**Inside colour** | Orange, red or yellow<br>Orange, red or yellow | Orange, red or yellow<br>Orange, red or yellow | Approved colour |
| **Sizing "adults"**<br>**Sizing "children"** | Universal over 41 kg<br>Universal under 41 kg | Universal | Chest size and/or weight<br>Weight only 3 categories |
| **Type of boating** | Abandon ship emergency use | Abandon ship emergency use in sheltered waters | General boating<br>For constant wear where risk exists |
| **Turns unconscious person face up in water?** | Yes | Yes, for most people | No<br>Provides flotation only |
| **Advantages** | High buoyancy, turning ability in rough weather. Simple to put on. | Reduce buoyancy and turning ability. Simple to put on. | Comfortable. Wide range of styles/sizes available for recreational boating |
| **Disadvantages** | Bulky and uncomfortable | Bulky and uncomfortable | No turning ability |

# Navigation lights

If a boat is operated between sunset and sunrise or in restricted visibility it must display navigation lights. It is illegal to operate a personal watercraft after dark unless properly fitted with navigation lights that meet current Collision Regulations. The various options are illustrated.

A mast head light shows forward through the same 225° arc of light as the red and green side lights. The stern light shows aft through the remaining 135° arc. With both masthead and the stern lights turned on other boaters can see white light all the way around your boat.

## Navigation lights for power-driven vessels

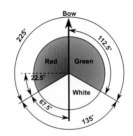

Coverage of arc of lights

**OPTION 1:** Navigation lights for small motor vessels less than 20m long, when under way.

**OPTION 2:** Navigation lights for small motor vessels less than 20m long, when under way.

**OPTION 3:** Motor boats less than 12m long, when under way.

## Navigation lights for sailing vessels

**OPTION 1:** Sailing vessels less than 7m long, when under way. A flashlight showing a white light, exhibited in sufficient time to prevent collision.

**OPTION 2:** Sailing vessel when under way.

**Option 3:** Sailing vessel when under way. These two lights shall not be exhibited in conjunction with the combined red, green and white lantern, i.e., Option 4.

**Option 4:** Sailing vessels less than 20m long.

## Navigation lights non-powered vessel

**OPTION 1:** A vessel under oars, when under way. A flashlight showing a white light, exhibited in sufficient time to prevent collision.

**OPTION 2:** A vessel under oars, when under way.

**ARM SIGNAL:** Raise and lower out-stretched arms repeatedly.

**DISTRESS CLOTH:** To attract attention: spread on cabin or deck top, or fly from mast.

**DYE MARKER**

## Distress signals

There are four types of distress flares approved by Transport Canada. Provided a water-tight flashlight is carried, flares are not required on boats up to 6 metres in length. They are required on larger boats. A small boat operator should consider carrying such equipment as a safety precaution. The most popular flare, Type-B, fires two or more stars high in the air and is an excellent distress signal. Carry the minimum number required by the regulations.

The cost of flares is small compared to their value for safety. They must be Canadian approved. Daytime signals include mirrors, distress flags and signals such as floating or hand-held orange smoke flares. Night-time signals include hand-held flares, pistol parachute flares, red aerial flares and flashlights. At any time flames on deck constitute a distress signal.

Learn how to signal a distress situation in all conditions, day or night. Buy the Distress Signalling DVD and book from Canadian Power and Sail Squadrons. 1-888-CPS-BOAT

**SOUND SIGNALLING DEVICES:** The sound-signalling device can be a pealess whistle, compressed gas horn or an electric horn.

**EPIRB:** Emergency Position Indicating Radio Beacon.

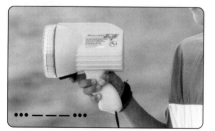

**FLASHLIGHT:** Almost every pleasure craft requires a watertight flashlight or flares. In the event of an electrical failure, a watertight flashlight may be your only means of signalling for help. Or signal SOS repeatedly.

**MIRROR**

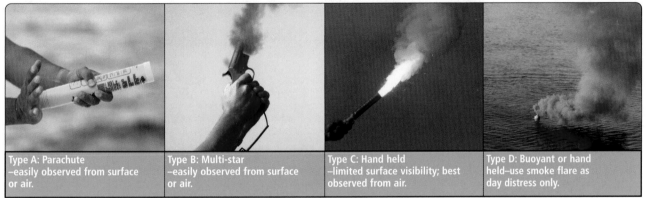

| Type A: Parachute –easily observed from surface or air. | Type B: Multi-star –easily observed from surface or air. | Type C: Hand held –limited surface visibility; best observed from air. | Type D: Buoyant or hand held–use smoke flare as day distress only. |

Note: Some type B flares project only one star at a time. When using this single star type, 2 flares must be fired within 15 seconds of each other—you will need double the number of cartridges to meet the regulations.

## General information for flares

- Read and understand the instructions
- They are valid only for four years from date of manufacture
- Hold lighted flares over the downwind side of the boat
- Do not point them at anyone, and hold away from your body
- Store in a watertight container, in a dry location
- Flares should be readily accessible for use
- They are to be used only in case of an emergency

## Optional equipment

The boat should be equipped with a buoyant, watertight emergency kit. Depending on the type of boat and the area in which it is being used, this kit might contain:

- a flashlight
- a whistle
- a knife
- a first aid kit
- emergency rations and drinking water

Other items might be carried in addition to the kit such as:

- anchor and anchor line
- binoculars
- charts
- depth sounder
- docking lines; fenders
- signal mirror
- thermos flask
- dry clothing

- shear and cotter pins if the engine needs them

## Radar reflectors

Vessels less than 20 m (65'7") in length or that are constructed primarily of non-metallic materials usually must have radar reflectors. But, radar reflectors are not needed:

- when they are not essential to the safety of the vessel,
- when the small size of the vessel makes it impractical,
- if the boat operating away from areas of radar navigation makes compliance impractical.

If properly positioned, radar reflectors help larger, less manoeuvrable vessels detect your presence on their radar screens. They should be located above all super-structures and at least 4 m (13'1") above

the water where possible.

As the cost and size of VHF Radios have decreased considerably in the last few years, a prudent boat operator will also carry this equipment.

Remember the radio operator must be certified. If a boat is in serious trouble or if someone on the boat is in serious trouble, the distress call is "Mayday" spoken three times and followed with a short description of your distress. Cellular telephones and CB radios are also a consideration. In some areas dialling *16 will connect to an emergency service.

Canadian Power & Sail Squadrons offer Marine Radio (VHF), a course leading to a radiotelephone operator's restricted certificate. Just what you need to operate a VHF, MF or HF marine band radio.

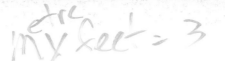

## SECTION 2: Equipping your boat

From the four possible answers given below, select the one you think is most nearly correct.

**1. A 7.0m boat must carry:** – 21 feet

   **A.** a magnetic compass

   **B.** three fire extinguishers

   **C.** a sound-signaling device

   **D.** a lifebuoy with a self-igniting light

**2. Every life jacket or PFD must be:**

   **A.** the same colour as your boat

   **B.** of the approved type

   **C.** carefully locked away when on board

   **D.** carried only in rough weather

**3. Canadian approved lifejackets:**

   **A.** make good fenders

   **B.** should be worn by children and non-swimmers

   **C.** never wear out

   **D.** always carry self-igniting lights

**4. Navigation lights on pleasure boats are:**

   **A.** red, white and blue

   **B.** red, green and yellow

   **C.** red, green and white

   **D.** green and yellow

**5. The starboard navigation light on a boat that is 6.0m long is:**

   **A.** red

   **B.** green

   **C.** yellow

   **D.** white

**6. A boat that is 6.0m long must have one approved life jacket or PFD of appropriate size for each:**

   **A.** available seat

   **B.** paying passenger

   **C.** child under age 12

   **D.** person on board

7. **The flares carried on a boat are valid:**
   A. for 4 years from date of manufacture
   B. for 4 years from date of purchase
   C. for 4 boating seasons
   D. for the life of the original owners

8. **The VHF radio installed in a boat requires:**
   A. proof of ownership of the set
   B. that the operator understands Morse code
   C. that the set be inspected annually
   D. that the operator be certified

9. **A sailboat may carry on the mast instead of the usual navigation lights:**
   A. combination light with red, yellow and green sectors
   B. combination light with white, green and red sectors
   C. a red light above a white light
   D. a white light above a red light

10. **Which piece of equipment must a vessel less than 12 metres in length carry?**
    A. a power fire hose
    B. a fire axe
    C. a sound-signaling device
    D. a certified marine toilet

| Answers | | |
|---|---|---|
| 1-c | 4-c | 8-d |
| 2-b | 5-b | 9-b |
| 3-b | 6-d | 10-c |
| | 7-a | |

# Safety awareness

Despite all the precautions that may be taken, difficulties will arise. They can be divided into two types: those that affect the crew and those that affect the boat.

## Precautions for passengers and crew

The most common accident to passengers and crew is falling. The likelihood of this happening can be greatly reduced. When your passengers move remind them to check for good footing and to hold a solid part of the boat. Remember the old saying: "Sailors were given two hands: one for the boat, and one for themselves." Move from hand hold to hand hold.

A cold, wet boater is uncomfortable and inefficient. Protection against cold can be special clothing such as wet or dry suits and immersion or survival clothing or as simple as multiple layers of dry clothing with a weather-proof outer shell.

## Falling overboard

Do not stand up in a small boat or ride on the sides, seat backs, or bow. These actions make a fall overboard more likely. If you let go of the tiller or the wheel of many boats, the boat will snap into a tight corner. Anyone sitting above the

gunwale will be thrown out. Anyone still in the boat will be pinned to the inside hull. It may be some time before the boat can be stopped especially if the operator is not tethered to the ignition switch.

If you need to change position in a small boat, hold on to both sides (gunwales) and keep your weight low. Standing in a small boat to start the engine or land a fish, makes a fall overboard more likely.

## Overboard and recovery

The best advice with regard to falling overboard is DON'T. Forty per cent of all fatal boating accidents started with falling over the side. Most of the victims were not wearing PFDs or lifejackets. To get a person back on board a boat should have a boarding ladder, buoyant heaving line, transom platform or some other means for reboarding.

When someone falls overboard:
**1.** Sound an alarm, i.e., Shout *"OVERBOARD"*

**2.** Throw a buoyant object, such as a buoyant cushion, PFD or lifering to mark the spot and assist the person. If you throw the heaving line you will not have it to retrieve the person later.

**3.** Assign a person to keep sight of the person in the water. Use a flashlight at night.

**4.** Turn the boat back and approach the person with the boat facing upwind.

To avoid injury by the propeller, when alongside the person in distress, the engine must be switched off, **not just put into neutral.** Getting the person back on board may be difficult. If the boat has high sides it may be necessary to rig some sort of sling. If the boat is small it is best to bring the person in over the stern. An attempt to bring a person over the side of a small boat often results in capsizing or swamping.

Single person wearing a flotation device: fetal position

Two or more persons; huddle

It is difficult to remember all this during an emergency. The skipper and crew should practise 'Overboard' rescue procedures from time to time. **Do not practise with a person in the water;** 'a hat overboard' is a much safer routine.

## Surviving in cold water

Cold water shock causes more deaths than hypothermia. Canada's typically cold waters are especially dangerous if you are unexpectedly immersed in them. There

are four main stages to the body's reaction to cold water immersion:

**Stage One:** for the first three to five minutes after sudden immersion a person will gasp for breath. If gasping for breath with your head underwater it could be your last gasp. Wear a PFD. If you are rescuing a person who has been in cold water for 3 – 5 minutes, you may find the person is not able to use his hands to help. After 15 – 20 minutes the person will not be able to help at all. After 3 – 5

Try to climb onto any nearby floating object

## Effects of Immersion in Cold Water

| Water Temperature °C | Exhaustion or Unconsciousness | Expected Time of Incipient Death (Non-drowning) |
|---|---|---|
| 0° | Less than 15 minutes | Less than one hour |
| 1 to 5° | 15 to 30 minutes | 30 to 90 minutes |
| 5 to 10° | 30 to 60 minutes | 2 to 4 hours |
| 10 to 15° | 1 to 2 hours | 3 to 6 hours |
| 15 to 20° | 2 to 7 hours | 5 to 10 hours |
| 20 to 27° | 3 to 12 hours | More than 8 hours |
| over 27° | Indefinite | Indefinite |

minutes of gasping a person will experience uncontrollable hyperventilation. This can cause dizziness, confusion and muscle spasms. There will be a dramatic rise in heart rate and blood pressure. If the victim has a heart condition they may be susceptible to cardiac arrest when suddenly immersed in water of 10° C or lower.

**Stage Two:** from three to thirty minutes limbs will cool. The ability of your muscles to contract, grip strength and manual dexterity will become impaired quickly. The body becomes "numb" with cold. Even experienced swimmers have great difficulties swimming more than a few meters. Increased swimming efforts lead to greater body cooling. You can see why in stages one and two it is difficult, if not impossible, to locate and don a PFD. This is why it is important to always wear your PFD.

**Stage Three:** a drop in deep body temperature from 37° C to just 35° C greatly reduces your ability to think or move. The disabilities of stage three make self rescue virtually impossible.

**Stage Four:** post rescue collapse may occur after someone is rescued, if they are warmed or moved too quickly. A stroke or heart attack may occur.

# Hypothermia

Hypothermia is a condition in which the body temperature drops below normal. If you compare the two, you can see that Cold Water Shock leads to hypothermia. Hypothermia can happen quickly when a person is immersed in cold water. Hypothermia can also come on slower when a person is cold or cold and wet. Hypothermia can place the body in a state of shock. A quick rescue is essential. Shock slows normal body functions so self help is impossible and outside care is mandatory.

The main areas of heat loss are the head and neck, the sides of the chest, and the lower abdomen. A person overboard will become hypothermic slower if the head is kept dry and arm pits and groin are kept closed.

**Symptoms are:**

1. **Early:** shivering and slurred speech, conscious but withdrawn;
2. **Intermediate:** slow and weak pulse, slow respiration, lacks co-ordination, irrational, confused and sleepy;
3. **Final:** weak, irregular or absent pulse or respiration, loss of consciousness.

A person suffering from hypothermia must be treated gently, sheltered from the cold, and provided dry clothing. Warm the body gradually. This must not be done by rubbing the limbs or the surface of the body. If the person asks for a beverage, offer warm water, milk or juice. Foods high in carbohydrates, such as honey or candy bars, will help. Never give alcohol, or hot stimulants, such as coffee, tea or cocoa. Call for help, including medical assistance, if necessary.

When aiding a person in stage 2 hypothermia professional medical help should be considered.

A person who has suffered stage 3 should be removed to a hospital as quickly and gently as possible.

# Illness

Any combination of motion, sunlight, wind, noise, waves and alcohol may cause seasickness. This results in loss of balance and co-ordination. Judgement, response time, and even eyesight and hearing can be impaired.

Few passengers think about this, and rely on the operator to do everything. But what happens if the operator is taken seriously ill? If those on board have been properly instructed, they should be able to take control of the boat.

There are non-drug ways of controlling seasickness:

- Give the sick person the helm with instructions to watch the horizon
- Chew ginger root
- Find and press lightly the pressure point on the inside of your wrist about where you look for a pulse

## Carbon monoxide poisoning

Carbon monoxide produced by gasoline and diesel engines is very toxic. It can cause headache, dizziness, loss of consciousness and, eventually, death. Since carbon monoxide is colourless, odourless and is approximately the same weight as air, the best prevention is to ensure that the boat is well ventilated.

Every year, people on or around boats are overcome by the effects of carbon monoxide.

Boaters need to take steps to prevent carbon monoxide problems:
- have regular, professional, boat inspections
- install and maintain carbon monoxide detectors in living spaces
- check regularly for exhaust leaks from CO sources: engines, generators, propane appliances
- be aware of boat design areas where fumes may gather
- warn swimmers to stay away from stern while generators and engines are in operation.
- Don't "teak surf" – hanging off the back of the swim platform when the engine is on and the boat is in motion

## Rendering first aid

First aid uses available material to give aid to an injured or suddenly ill person. First aid should be administered to the best of your ability. All those who go boating can benefit from taking a Red Cross, or St. John Ambulance First Aid Course.

Medical problems most likely to occur when boating are cuts and bruises, dehydration, heat exhaustion, sunburn, sea-sickness and hypothermia. A first-aid kit should contain: band-aids, bandages, sea-sickness remedies, sun-burn lotion, disinfectant and should always be carried on board.

More serious medical problems can seldom be dealt with on board. If the person is not breathing, unconscious or has severe bleeding, emergency action must be taken. This may be an appropriate time for a MAYDAY, 911 or *16 (in some areas) call to get help faster. Otherwise, the person should be made as comfortable as possible and taken to shore for medical assistance without delay.

## Precautions for the boat

The three areas of difficulty most likely to affect a boat are mechanical failure, collision with some other object such as another boat, log, or rock and deterioration in the weather. In general, in case of trouble, reduce speed until the problem has been found.

## Mechanical failure

The likelihood of mechanical failure can be reduced by regular maintenance of the boat. The most frequent cause of engine failure is the lack of fuel.

When planning a trip use the three thirds method. Plan on one third to get you to your destination, one third to get you back and one third for reserve. If the weather changes you may need more fuel than planned. Aircraft pilots must have significant fuel in the tanks on landing. This is a good plan to copy.

The fuel tank vent should also be checked to make sure it is open and clear. If the boat has run through rough water, dirt in the tank may have been stirred up. So check the fuel filters.

Overheating may be due to a faulty water pump impeller, or blockage of the water intake by weeds or a plastic bag.

A poorly maintained ignition system may cause engine trouble. This can be prevented by proper maintenance. Clean or replace spark plugs in the spring.

Check high tension leads, and replace

worn points, if fitted.

If nothing can be done to restart the engine and the water is shallow enough, lower the anchor and try to attract attention for assistance from a passing boat.

## Hull leaks

If there is an unusually large amount of water in the bilge, the boat has probably sprung a leak. If it is not found, fixed quickly and the water bailed out, the boat may sink. Unless there has been a collision, or the boat has run aground, the leak may be caused by:

- the plug coming out of the drain hole
- a through-hull fitting breaking off
- an engine hose coming loose
- a defective self-bailer

Check all these areas quickly. Generally, a leak can be fixed temporarily with clamps or tape. Spare clamps, tape and plugs should be kept on board. The leak may have to be fixed from outside the boat. In this case someone may have to go into the water. If this is necessary, a safety line should always be attached to the person and to the boat. Where practical the person in the water should wear a PFD. A means for reboarding must be available.

## Collision

There is seldom an excuse for a collision. It can almost always be avoided by keeping a good look-out, paying attention to steering and carefully reading the charts to check your position. Reduce speed after heavy rains. Storm water may stir up logs and debris.

When a boat has collided with another boat, hit a log or run aground, check the bilge immediately for water. Also check

the hull for damage. It is not advisable to push a boat off a rock and into deep water if there is a hole in the hull. Check the engine, propeller and steering to be sure the boat can still be manoeuvred.

## Fog

If possible, stay out of fog. If fog rolls in:
- Turn on the navigation lights
- Proceed at a safe speed for the prevailing conditions
- Keep a sharp look-out
- Sound the fog signal
- Raise a RADAR reflector

If you are going at a safe speed in fog you will be able to stop before hitting anything that appears out of the fog.

If the fog gets too thick, stop until visibility improves.

## Bad weather

If the weather turns bad, proceed at a safe speed for the prevailing conditions. Put on lifejackets and head for safety at an angle to the waves. Secure loose equipment. Switch to a full fuel tank. Keep all weight low. In a small boat sit passengers on the floor near the centre line. If necessary,

anchor until the weather improves.

## Capsizing/swamping/sinking

Overloading, mechanical failure, or poor weather may capsize, swamp or sink a boat. If a boat capsizes or is swamped, don lifejackets, make sure that everyone is accounted for and call for help if possible. Usually it is best to stay with the boat. There is a much better chance of being seen and rescued. If the boat sinks, cling to whatever floating debris can be found and, if possible, tie it together as a float.

## Falling from a PWC

PWCs are equipped with one of the following:
- A lanyard attached to the rider, that will shut off the engine in the event the rider falls off.
- Automatic idle, which will cause the PWC to circle slowly in the area until the rider can reboard.

If you fall off, swim back to the PWC, reboard carefully and reattach the lanyard if applicable. Restart the engine and take care.

## Getting help

If problems arise, help can often be summoned by attracting the attention of passing boats. This may be done by waving flags or raising and lowering your arms. If this is not successful, flares may be fired. The VHF radiotelephone, CB or cellular phone may be used to summon assistance. It is illegal to send false messages. Do not call for help unless you need it.

## Rendering assistance

All boaters should watch for distress signals from other boats. You are obliged to stop and render assistance if required. This applies to all boaters who are at, or near, the scene, whether they are directly involved or not. Of primary importance in a rescue, when aiding others, you must not put your own boat or persons on your boat at risk. This is similar to aiding a swimmer at a pool or a beach. Offer rescue with a towel, paddle, oar, or stick but never your hand.

## Accident reports[2]

The Criminal Code of Canada looks on boating accidents much the same as automobile accidents. If you are involved, you must stop, give your name and address, and offer assistance.

**If involved in an accident:**

- that results in a personal injury requiring medical treatment beyond first aid but not admittance to a hospital OR
- that causes property damage estimated at more than $2500

The boat operator must complete a Boating Accident Report Form and forward it to the Office of Boating Safety of TC,

not later than 14 days after the accident.

**If involved in an accident that results in:**

- a fatality
- injury to a person requiring admittance to a hospital, OR
- property damage greater than $5000,
The boat operator must report the accident to the local police authority as soon as possible.

## Fire precautions

Fire on board is a serious matter. Often there is nowhere to go but into the water. Fire requires three things to sustain it: fuel, heat, and oxygen. With fuel on board and oxygen in the air great care must be taken. Be sure that the third item, heat, does not contact the other

two. Sources of heat on a boat include careless smoking, electrical sparks and open flames. Damp charcoal, oily rags and other similar materials stored in a closed container can start burning by themselves – spontaneous combustion.

Fuels such as gasoline and propane can be very dangerous. Their vapours are heavier than air and can drift down into the lower area of the boat, the bilge. Here they may form an explosive mixture with air.

---

[2] where an agreement has been reached between Federal and Provincial Governments.

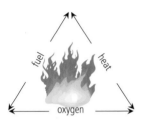

## Ventilation

If the engine or fuel space is enclosed it must be properly ventilated with the minimum of two ventilation cowls. One brings in fresh air and one takes air and vapours out. A blower should also be fitted to help expel vapours.

## Backfire flame arrestors

Engines may backfire and the fire from these explosions can come out through the

⚠️ Never store oily rags on board. Before starting your engine, operate the ventilation blower for at least four minutes.

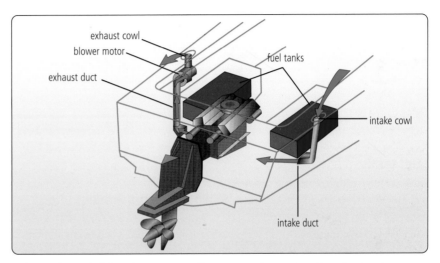

carburetor instead of the exhaust system. All motorboats, except outboards and diesels, must have a clean, well-secured, backfire flame arrestor system on each carburetor.

## Ignition protection

Automobile engines have been installed in some boats. An unknowing handyman may have replaced marine parts with less expensive automotive versions. This can be explosively dangerous. Be sure that ignition protected marine rated parts are used in your boat.

If a small outboard unit, such as used when trolling, is stored inside the boat, take care that neither raw gasoline, nor its vapour can accumulate in the bilge.

## Drip pans

These should be fitted under the updraft carburetors of inboard gasoline engines.

## Fuel tanks

Fixed fuel tanks and lines should be installed and maintained and fuelling conducted so as to prevent leakage of fuel and spillage into the hull or into the water.

## Refuelling

Refuelling precautions are discussed later in the manual.

## Fuel-burning appliances

Combustion stoves and heaters must be installed to allow full circulation of air around them. Propane tanks and auxiliary fuel containers must be stored outside the boat where they can be fully ventilated. Turn propane and gas stoves off at the tank when not in use. No unattended open flame is permitted on a gas system

Woodwork, curtains and other flammable material must be efficiently shielded from hot pipes and other sources of heat.

## Fire extinguishers

Because a fire requires fuel, heat and oxygen to sustain it, the removal of any one will bring the fire under control. In most cases that is achieved by using a fire extinguisher to cut off the air supply or cool the fire. Read and understand the instructions on the fire extinguisher. Once a fire starts it is too late. Act immediately. Don't hesitate! If a fire starts, grab the extinguisher, activate it and direct it at

the base of the flames. Use short bursts and sweep the foam from side to side. If under way, and a fire starts, stop the boat and position it so that the fire is downwind. Wind from the boat's motion will fan the flames. If not already wearing them, put on lifejackets. Turn off any fuel supply if possible.

## Types of extinguisher

All fire extinguishers must be approved by Transport Canada, Underwriters' Laboratories of Canada or, in the United States, by the U.S. Coast Guard. They should be inspected regularly. They should be replaced or recharged when the indicator shows that they are no longer fully charged.

Fire extinguishers may contain foam, carbon dioxide or dry chemicals. Letters "A," "B" or "C" on the label indicate their intended use. Never use water on a gasoline, oil, grease or electrical fire. Water can be used to extinguish burning wood, mattresses, rags, rubbish, and alcohol. Fire extinguishers using dry chemicals should be shaken every few weeks, to ensure the chemicals do not

pack into a solid mass. Vertical mounting of dry chemicals is required.

The letters A, B or C which appear on the label, represent the class of fire the extinguisher is designed for. It is important to be familiar with their operation and to

place them where they are readily available for use. The 5 and 10BC extinguishers mentioned in the previous chapter are for fires experienced on small boats.

## Equipment required

All boats should have at least one fire extinguisher. A PWC is exempt from carrying a fire extinguisher only if there is no provision for storage. Cautious boaters have two.

 **A** combustible solid (wood, paper, etc.)

 **B** combustible liquid (gas, oil, etc.)

**C** electrical

Even though the boat may be equipped with an automatic extinguishing system, you are still required to carry the required number of portable extinguishers. It is important to be familiar with their operation, and to place them where they are readily available.

### SECTION 3: Safety Awareness

From the four possible answers given below, select the one you think is most nearly correct.

1.  **The most common boating accident to passengers and crew is the result of:**
    A.  collisions with other boats
    B.  heart attacks
    C.  persons falling
    D.  boats running aground

2.  **Fire extinguishers on a boat must be approved by:**
    A.  the Ministry of the Environment
    B.  any local office of Canada Customs
    C.  the Association of Marine Firefighters
    D.  Transport Canada

3.  **In what percentage of fatal boating accidents is falling overboard the main cause?**
    A.  10%
    B.  40%
    C.  60%
    D.  50%

4.  **When rescuing someone from the water, you should approach the victim slowly in:**
    A.  an upwind direction
    B.  a downwind direction
    C.  across the wind
    D.  at an angle across the wind

5.  **In water, with a temperature below 5°C (40°F), unconsciousness from hypothermia can occur in:**
    A.  10 minutes
    B.  30 minutes
    C.  60 minutes
    D.  5 minutes

6. **Which of the following should NOT be given to a person suffering from hypothermia?**
   A. warm milk
   B. brandy
   C. candy bars
   D. honey

7. **If thick fog rolls in unexpectedly when you are out in a boat, you should:**
   A. increase speed to get home as quickly as possible
   B. send up a distress flare
   C. stop until it clears
   D. call the Coast Guard

8. **In rough weather, the safest course to steer is:**
   A. broadside to the waves
   B. at an angle into the waves
   C. downwind
   D. directly into the waves

9. **If you see another boat in trouble, you must:**
   A. Leave quickly, so as not to be involved.
   B. Stay back, and watch what happens.
   C. Render assistance, if possible.
   D. Carry on fishing.

10. **A condition in which the body temperature drops below normal is called:**
    A. suffocation
    B. exhaustion
    C. hypothermia
    D. influenza

| Answers | 4-a | 8-b |
|---------|-----|-----|
| 1-c | 5-b | 9-c |
| 2-d | 6-b | 10-c |
| 3-b | 7-c | |

# Marine rules of the road

## Collision Regulations

A power-driven vessel means any vessel propelled by machinery as described in the Collision Regulations. Therefore, when a sailboat uses its engine, it is legally a power boat. This is true even if it is using its sails while using its engine. As a power boat, it is subject to "power boat" regulations.

## Regulations

The Introduction page lists seven rules, regulations and codes that control all boating. A word of encouragement: You will not be expected to quote all the navigation rules. However, no matter where you do your boating, others have the right to assume that you know what you are doing. When you take control of a boat you are responsible for its operation and your actions. These rules are based on common sense. They are designed to avoid collisions on the water, and must be obeyed. They are simple to understand provided that the nautical terminology for "left" and "right" is fully understood.

When facing forward in a boat, the left side of the boat is the port side. The right side is starboard. Remember from chapter 2 Navigational Lights. The red light is seen on the port side from dead ahead to just behind the port beam. The green light is seen over the same arc on the starboard side.

The arc displaying the red light shows an approaching boat that you have the right of way. The other boat must keep clear of your boat. The green arc informs

another boat that it has the right of way; you must take precautions. For this reason, the green arc is known as the danger zone.

Because they are less manoeuvrable, sailboats and boats propelled by oars or paddles have the right-of-way over motorboats. The only exception is when a sailboat or other non-powered boat overtakes a motorboat.

Pleasure craft less than 20 metres, whether under power or sail, must take early and substantial action to keep clear of 'commercial' vessels engaged in fishing, where the gear being used restricts their manoeuvrability. Fishing boats that have right of way have nets, trawls or other fishing apparatus which restricts their manoeuvrability.

Since they cannot manoeuvre quickly or easily and since they must have the

deep water, large deep-draft vessels in narrow channels or traffic lanes also have the right-of-way.

## Sound signals for poor visibility

Sound signals are also used when visibility is poor. A sailboat sounds one long blast, followed by two short blasts, every two minutes. A power boat sounds one long blast every two minutes when moving through the water and two long blasts every two minutes when stopped.

## Manoeuvring and sound signals

The operator of a give-way vessel must take early and substantial action to keep well clear of the other boat as illustrated.

## Overtaking

Stand-on
vessel being overtaken

Great Lakes Rules
"I want to pass
you on your
port side."
2 short blasts
(1 sec.)

Great Lakes Rules
"I want to pass
you on your
starboard side."
1 short blast
(1 sec.)

"Proceed"
2 short blasts
(1 sec.)

"Proceed."
1 short blast
(1 sec.)

International
Rules
"I am altering
my course to
port."
2 short blasts
(1 sec.)

International
Rules
"I am altering my
course to
starboard."
1 short blast
(1 sec.)

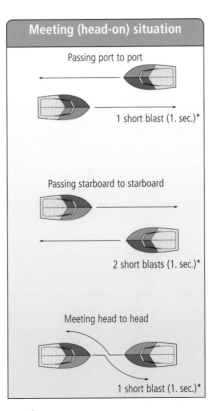

Give-way
vessel overtaking

The same rules apply to sailing vessels

## Meeting (head-on) situation

Passing port to port

1 short blast (1. sec.)*

Passing starboard to starboard

2 short blasts (1. sec.)*

Meeting head to head

1 short blast (1. sec.)*

## Motorboats must stay clear of boats under sail

Stand-on vessel

holds course and speed

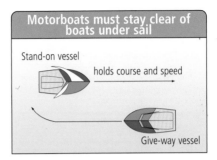

Give-way vessel

## Crossing situation

Stand-on vessel
(boat with the
right-of-way)
holds course
and speed

1 short blast
(1. sec.)*

Danger zone
112.5°

Give-way
vessel

1 short blast (1. sec.)*

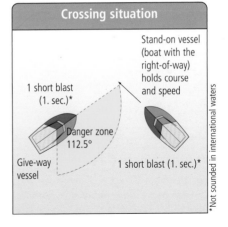

*Not sounded in international waters

## Sailing vessel

1. When each sailing vessel has the wind on a different side, the vessel which has the wind on the port side shall keep out of the way of the other.

2. When both sailing vessels have the wind on the same side, the vessel which is to windward shall keep out of the way of the vessel which is to leeward.

3. If a sailing vessel with the wind on the port side sees a sailing vessel to windward and cannot determine with certainty whether the other sailing vessel has the wind on the port or the starboard side, it shall keep out of the way of the other.

Note: The windward side shall be deemed to be the side opposite to that on which the mainsail is carried.

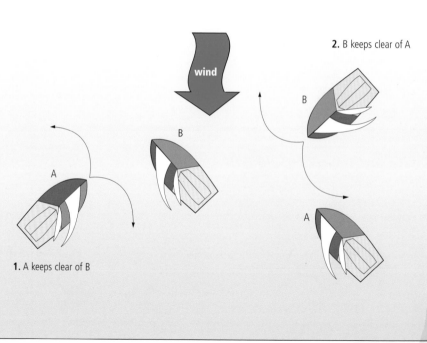

**2.** B keeps clear of A

**1.** A keeps clear of B

**CHAPTER 4: Marine Rules of the Road (Collision Regulations)**

From the four possible answers given below, select the one you think is most nearly correct.

1. **If two power boats are approaching each other head on, or nearly so, they should:**
   A. stop
   B. turn to starboard
   C. turn to port
   D. increase speed to pass each other as quickly as possible

2. **When one boat overtakes another, the overtaking boat:**
   A. must pass to the port side
   B. must pass to the starboard side
   C. may pass on either side, if safe to do so
   D. must sound three short blasts

3. **Which of the following always has the right of way in a narrow channel?**
   A. sailboat that is motoring
   B. a large commercial vessel
   C. a sailboat that is sailing
   D. a boat less than 5.5m long

4. **Navigation rules apply:**
   A. only to commercial vessels
   B. to all boats
   C. only when a boat is under way
   D. to all boats, except sailboats

5. **When being overtaken, a boat must:**
   A. alter course to starboard
   B. alter course to port
   C. maintain course and speed
   D. slow down or stop

6. **In poor visibility, the sound signal that a moving power boat should make every two minutes is:**
   A. two short blasts
   B. two long blasts
   C. one long and two short blasts
   D. one long blast

7. **Your danger zone is an arc:**
   A. from ahead to 112.5° starboard
   B. from ahead to 112.5° port
   C. where your white light is visible
   D. 112.5° each side of dead astern

8. **When two power boats are on crossing courses, the give-way boat is:**
   A. the one with the wind on starboard
   B. the one to the right of the other
   C. the one to the left of the other
   D. the faster boat

9. **When a small sailboat meets a large commercial craft in a narrow channel, it should:**
   A. Give two blasts on the horn, and stand on
   B. Give way
   C. Give way only if the wind is on the port side
   D. Give way only if the wind is on the starboard side

10. **A red light is displayed on a small power boat:**
    A. on the port side
    B. on the starboard side
    C. at all times when under way
    D. only when at anchor

| Answers | 4-b | 8-c |
| --- | --- | --- |
| 1-b | 5-c | 9-b |
| 2-c | 6-d | 10-a |
| 3-b | 7-a | |

# The Canadian Aids to Navigation System

The Aids to Navigation system is made up of floating buoys, lights, and land-based markers that assists the operator in determining his position. It displays the best, preferred route and warns the boater of dangers and obstructions.

## Buoys

A buoy is a floating aid to navigation. Lighthouses or other navigation markers on land are not buoys. Canadian Aids to Navigation system includes three types of buoy as well as other waterway markers and flags.

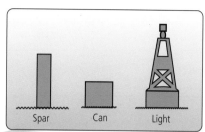

## Lateral buoys

These buoys can be green with flat tops and given odd numbers. Or they can be red with pointed tops and given even numbers. The shape of the top of the buoy is important. Sometimes it is difficult to identify colour at a distance, in poor lighting conditions or if you or your crew is one of the many people who are red/green colour blind.

Green buoys are referred to as "port-hand buoys" because they are kept to port when going upstream or into harbour. Red buoys are referred to as "starboard-hand buoys" because they are kept to starboard when going upstream or into harbour. A useful phrase is: "Even points are red on the right returning". This indicates that pointed buoys, coloured red, have even numbers on them and are kept to the right side of the boat when returning to harbour or going upstream. A shorter aid to remember is this: "Red, right, returning."

When leaving harbour or going downstream the situation is reversed. Green buoys are kept to starboard and red buoys are kept to port.

Some 'spar buoys' now have lights too. Larger buoys called structural or pillar buoys may take many shapes. See illustration. Red buoys may have a small pointed structure on them called a "topmark." Green buoys may have a "topmark." It is a flat-topped cylinder. When these buoys are lighted, the light is red or green to match the buoy's colour. These buoys are either flashing - (Fl)4s, or quick flashing - (Q)1s.

Red and white vertically striped buoys called "fairway buoys" mark the middle of the channel, and can be passed on either side.

Red and green horizontally banded buoys called "bifurcation buoys" show where a channel divides. The shape and colour at the top indicate the 'preferred' channel to port or to starboard when going upstream.

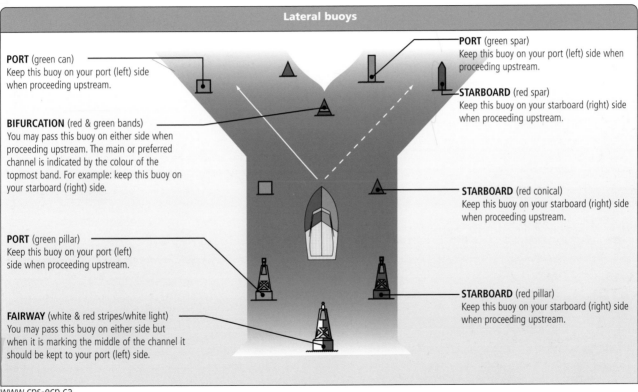

**Lateral buoys**

**PORT** (green can)
Keep this buoy on your port (left) side when proceeding upstream.

**BIFURCATION** (red & green bands)
You may pass this buoy on either side when proceeding upstream. The main or preferred channel is indicated by the colour of the topmost band. For example: keep this buoy on your starboard (right) side.

**PORT** (green pillar)
Keep this buoy on your port (left) side when proceeding upstream.

**FAIRWAY** (white & red stripes/white light)
You may pass this buoy on either side but when it is marking the middle of the channel it should be kept to your port (left) side.

**PORT** (green spar)
Keep this buoy on your port (left) side when proceeding upstream.

**STARBOARD** (red spar)
Keep this buoy on your starboard (right) side when proceeding upstream.

**STARBOARD** (red conical)
Keep this buoy on your starboard (right) side when proceeding upstream.

**STARBOARD** (red pillar)
Keep this buoy on your starboard (right) side when proceeding upstream.

# Cardinal buoys

There are four cardinal buoys: North, East, South and West. Named for the four cardinal points of the compass, cardinal buoys indicate the location of the safest and deepest water. The buoys are flat-topped and painted with yellow and black horizontal bands. Structural cardinal buoys may have a topmark that is made up of two black cones. If lighted, the cardinal buoys have a white light. The pattern of colours on the buoy, the pattern of the cones and the flash of the light show whether safe water lies north, south, east or west of it.

Note:

- Not all buoys are fitted with lights and topmarks.
- It is essential that this buoyage system be used in conjunction with the nautical charts.

## Cardinal buoys

N (Q) 1s

W Q(9) 15s    DANGER    Q(3) 10s E

S (Q(6) + LFl 15s)

Keep to the named side of all cardinal buoys. For example keep to the north of north cardinal buoys, keep to the east of east cardinal buoys and so on. Then the buoy will be between you and the danger. Consult your chart for details of the danger.

Memory aids

- The points of the topmark cones point toward the black parts of the buoy.
- The cones on the north cardinal point north and those on the south cardinal point south.
- The number of short light flashes in each group on the east, south and west cardinals is the same as the hour at the corresponding point on a clock face. The south Cardinal however, flashes six times followed by a long flash for quick identification

### Lights

**North:** White light; quick flashing every second.
**East:** White light; group quick flashing three every 10 seconds.
**South:** White light; group quick flashing six plus long flash
**West:** White light; group quick flashing nine every 15 seconds.

EAST    SOUTH    WEST

## Other waterway markers

These include buoys, lights and daybeacons. Other buoys indicate anchorages, moorings, controls, isolated hazards, etc. All of these markers and buoys are here for your safety.

> ⚠ It is illegal to tie your boat to a buoy or otherwise alter or obscure them from the public sight..

*Study !*

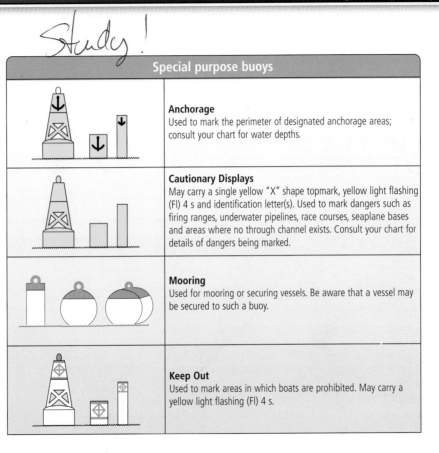

| Special purpose buoys | |
|---|---|
| | **Anchorage**<br>Used to mark the perimeter of designated anchorage areas; consult your chart for water depths. |
| | **Cautionary Displays**<br>May carry a single yellow "X" shape topmark, yellow light flashing (Fl) 4 s and identification letter(s). Used to mark dangers such as firing ranges, underwater pipelines, race courses, seaplane bases and areas where no through channel exists. Consult your chart for details of dangers being marked. |
| | **Mooring**<br>Used for mooring or securing vessels. Be aware that a vessel may be secured to such a buoy. |
| | **Keep Out**<br>Used to mark areas in which boats are prohibited. May carry a yellow light flashing (Fl) 4 s. |

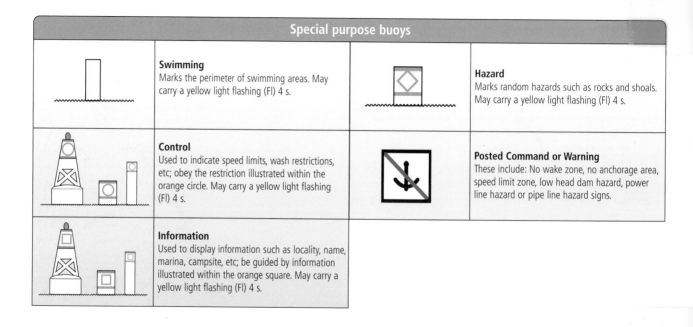

| Special purpose buoys | | |
|---|---|---|
| **Swimming** Marks the perimeter of swimming areas. May carry a yellow light flashing (Fl) 4 s. | **Hazard** Marks random hazards such as rocks and shoals. May carry a yellow light flashing (Fl) 4 s. |
| **Control** Used to indicate speed limits, wash restrictions, etc; obey the restriction illustrated within the orange circle. May carry a yellow light flashing (Fl) 4 s. | **Posted Command or Warning** These include: No wake zone, no anchorage area, speed limit zone, low head dam hazard, power line hazard or pipe line hazard signs. |
| **Information** Used to display information such as locality, name, marina, campsite, etc; be guided by information illustrated within the orange square. May carry a yellow light flashing (Fl) 4 s. | |

## Standard daybeacons

*DAY Beacon*

**Port Bifurcation/Junction**
Green reflective square on a white diamond with a red reflecting border. Marks a point where the channel divides and may be passed on either side. If the preferred channel is desired, the daybeacon should be kept on the vessel's port (left) side.

*Day Beacon*

**Port Hand**
Black or green square, centred on a white background, with a green reflecting border. May display an odd number of white reflecting material. When proceeding upstream, a port hand daybeacon must be kept on the vessel's port (left) side.

*Day Beacon*

**Starboard Bifurcation/Junction**
Red reflective triangle on a white diamond with a red reflecting border. Marks a point where the channel divides and may be passed on either side. If the preferred channel is desired, the daybeacon should be kept to the vessel's starboard (right) side.

**Starboard Hand**
A red triangle centred on a white background with a red reflecting border. May display an even number of white reflecting material. When proceeding upstream, must be kept on the vessel's starboard (right) side.

## Range

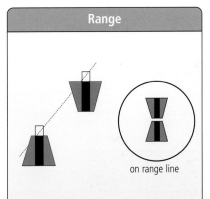

on range line

Consists of two or more fixed navigation marks situated some distance apart and at different elevations. May or may not be lighted. The shape and colours of the daymarks and the colours and characters of lights are advertised in the "List of Lights."

A range provides a leading line for navigators. When both marks are in line, the observer is on the recommended track. Consult the chart for the portion of channel serviced by the range.

## Diver's flag

When divers are underwater, two flags should be displayed. The accompanying vessel displays the international flag "A" (Alpha) which is blue and white. The exact location where the diver is working is marked by a white buoy that displays the diver's flag. The diver's flag is red with a white, diagonal stripe on it. If it carries a light, the light is yellow and is a flashing (Fl)4s light. A boat should not approach closer than 35 metres from either flag and pass at slow speed.

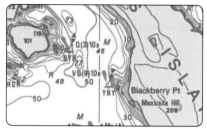

## Charts and chart reading

Charts are the road maps of the water and must be carried on board. They show water depths and the safest navigable route. Charts also provide locations of harbours, marinas, marine hazards and aids to navigation. They can be obtained from chart dealers or from the Canadian Hydrographic Office in Ottawa. Carry the most recent editions of the largest scale charts together with such other publications and documents as are required locally.

Where no charts are available, topographic maps may be used. These are intended for land use by the general public and show natural and artificial features, elevation contours, shoreline, rocks, land features above water and cultural features. They do not show marine aids to navigation, underwater hazards, boating channels or anchorages. They are published by Natural Resources Canada and some provincial authorities.

## The magnetic compass

The magnetic compass consists of a magnet mounted on a card that is marked from 000° to 360°. If the compass is mounted where it is not affected by iron, the boat's electrical or magnetic equipment, it will point to "magnetic" north. When a compass is being used it should be at least 3 metres away from all electric wires and equipment (radio, depth sounder), magnets (speakers and some speedometers) and steel or iron material (the engine, frying pan, flare gun). True north can be found by applying magnetic variation.

Local variation is marked inside the compass rose on a nautical chart.

## Finding position

Most aids to navigation, such as buoys and beacons, carry clearly visible numbers and/or letters and are similarly identified on the chart. When a marked buoy is seen, a boater can find its position from the chart. The compass can then be used for finding the direction to steer to get to the best fishing spot, best landing spot, your point of destination or the next marina.

To learn how to deal with compass variation and deviation, and how to plot a course. Take the CPS Boating or Piloting Course.

## CHAPTER 5: The Canadian Aids to Navigation System

From the four possible answers given below, select the one you think is most nearly correct.

1. **A boat's compass should be mounted:**
   A. close to the engine
   B. away from all magnetic influences
   C. near the depth finder
   D. next to the radio

2. **A small buoy with a red flag that has a white diagonal stripe on it indicates:**
   A. a rock
   B. a wreck
   C. the starting line for a race
   D. a diver is working below

3. **When going downstream, or leaving the harbour, green buoys are:**
   A. kept to port
   B. kept to starboard
   C. ignored
   D. passed on either side

4. **A buoy that is painted with red and white vertical stripes marks:**
   A. a wreck
   B. a fishing area
   C. the middle of a channel
   D. a shoal area

5. **If you see a boat displaying a blue-and-white flag, you should:**
   A. go in close to investigate
   B. lower your line, and start fishing
   C. keep well clear
   D. offer to help

**6. The magnetic compass:**
A. points to "true" north
B. points to "magnetic" north
C. is marked from 0 to 100
D. is not affected by iron objects on board

**7. A pointed spar buoy:**
A. is always kept to starboard
B. may be passed on either side
C. is kept to starboard when going upstream
D. is always kept to port

**8. A green pillar buoy displays:**
A. a blue flashing light
B. a red flashing light
C. a steady green light
D. a flashing green light

**9. A cardinal buoy is painted yellow above black. The safe water is:**
A. to the north
B. to the south
C. to the east
D. to the west

**10. A cardinal buoy displays as a topmark two cones, both pointing down. The safe water is:**
A. to the south
B. to the north
C. to the west
D. to the east

| Answers | 4-c | 8-d |
|---------|-----|------|
| 1-b | 5-c | 9-b |
| 2-d | 6-b | 10-a |
| 3-b | 7-c | |

# Trailering & transporting

Your boat trailer is an important part of your boating equipment. All too often the trailer does not receive the attention that it deserves and demands. Regular inspection and maintenance must be carried out. Care in hitching and towing is necessary. If these areas are neglected you may be endangering the safety of your boat, your car and other people.

## Trailer safety

The trailer must be strong enough to carry the weight that will be placed on it. The various types of boat and hull shapes will determine the trailer needed. The boat should fit snugly and there should be proper support for the bottom. If not

supported properly the hull could warp. Make sure the trailer lights work and carry spare light bulbs. Be sure you can see clearly. Check the car's side mirrors and check that the trailer license plate is visible.

## Trailer load

Your boat and its contents should weigh less than 80 per cent of the rated capacity of the trailer. Any items carried in the boat while trailered should be distributed evenly. Put heaviest items closer to the bottom. Gear should also be secured

carefully to keep from shifting. Transport Canada now specifies chains and tie downs.

Make sure the boat is properly secured to the trailer with tie-downs and a line from the boat's towing eye to the trailer's tongue or winch.

Trailer hitches come in a variety of shapes and sizes. Make sure you have a type that suits the towing vehicle and trailer and meets any legal requirements. The type that comes with the vehicle when you order it is the best. The trailer hitch should match the size of the ball.

Never use a ball hitch that is too small. There must be safety chains attaching the trailer to the vehicle. They must cross under the tongue of the trailer. If the hitch comes off the ball it should drop into this chain 'cradle' not onto the road.

## Tongue weight

Too much weight on the hitch will cause "tail dragging" of the towing vehicle and impaired steering. Too little weight on the hitch and the trailer will sway or "fishtail" possibly tossing the boat off the trailer. The whole assembly should be tongue

heavy so that the hitch carries approximately 10% of the gross weight. It is recommended that when the tow vehicle is one of the small or "compact" cars, the gross trailer weight should not exceed 450 kg, even though the ball and hitch have a higher capacity.

## On the road

Practise backing the trailer and become familiar with the performance of the vehicle before driving in traffic. Acceleration will be less and speed will be lost going uphill. Be very cautious passing other vehicles and

make sure you are well ahead before getting back in line. If braking is prolonged when going down hill there will be "brake fade" due to heat, and sudden stops may cause the trailer to jack-knife. If the loaded trailer weighs more than 1500 kg, it must be equipped with auxiliary brakes. Check provincial regulations for details.

## Launching

At the launch ramp, pull to one side and get ready. Take off the tie-downs and boat cover and raise the stern drive or engine. Disconnect the trailer's electrical system. This pause will allow the trailer's wheel bearings to cool. Make sure a line is attached to the boat ready for launching. Install the drain plug!

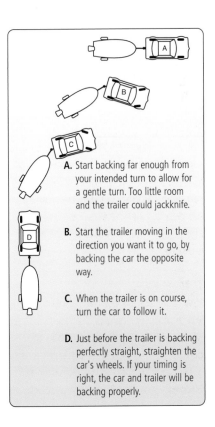

A. Start backing far enough from your intended turn to allow for a gentle turn. Too little room and the trailer could jackknife.

B. Start the trailer moving in the direction you want it to go, by backing the car the opposite way.

C. When the trailer is on course, turn the car to follow it.

D. Just before the trailer is backing perfectly straight, straighten the car's wheels. If your timing is right, the car and trailer will be backing properly.

Check the launch ramp for debris and slickness. If a sailboat is being launched with the mast up, care should be taken to avoid contact with overhead wires. Back slowly down the ramp. If you must leave the vehicle, make sure the brake is applied and the gearshift in park or in gear. If necessary, put chocks behind the wheels. Watch out for children. Make sure the drain plug is inserted. As you back, have a helper watch behind the boat. The helper's only job is to say 'STOP' if you are about to hit something, run over that little child or otherwise come to grief.

## Recovery

After the trailer has been backed down the ramp, the boat is run on to the centre line and winched into position. The steps described in the preceding paragraphs are then undertaken in reverse order. Wash the boat down and let dry. Don't infect other lakes with alien invasive species.

## Security

To protect your trailer from theft while parked, consider taking off one wheel and storing it in the car trunk. Add a hitch lock so that the trailer can't be easily towed away. If with a group, consider chaining several trailers together.

## CHAPTER 6: Trailering and transporting

From the four possible answers given below, select the one you think is most nearly correct.

1. **What per cent of the weight of a trailer and its load should be on the hitch?**
   A. 3%
   B. 5%
   C. 12%
   D. 10%

2. **Auxiliary brakes are required on a trailer that:**
   A. exceeds 1,500 kg in weight
   B. has 4 wheels
   C. weighs less than 1,500 kg
   D. is going more than 1,500 km

3. **The boat and its contents should weigh no more than:**
   A. 10% of the capacity of the trailer
   B. 50% of the capacity of the trailer
   C. 80% of the capacity of the trailer
   D. 100% of the capacity of the trailer

4. **The trailer is fitted with a 2" ball hitch. The ball must be:**
   A. 1 7/8"
   B. 1 3/4"
   C. 1 15/16"
   D. 2"

5. **Too much weight on the tongue will result in:**
   A. excessive wear on trailer tires
   B. fishtailing of the trailer
   C. jack-knifing whenever the vehicle stops
   D. tail dragging of the towing vehicle

| Answers | |
|---|---|
| 1-d | 4-d |
| 2-a | 5-d |
| 3-c | |

# Getting under way

## Before leaving the dock

The operator of a boat, even a small one, has certain responsibilities. The operator may be liable for the consequences if these responsibilities are neglected.

Before leaving the dock, the prudent boater will use a checklist to address the following:

- operator's PCOC, license
- check for gas fumes
- make sure there is adequate fuel on board
- make sure the electrical system is operational
- on a PWC and some boats check that the automatic stop switch lanyard is attached
- check that the required safety equipment is stowed in an accessible location

## Local regulations

There may be local port rules that must be observed.

## Weather conditions

Weather forecasts may be obtained from many sources: internet broadcast, radio, TV, newspapers, marine radio, directly from Environment Canada and, of course, by personal observation. Observe what is happening in a westerly direction where most weather patterns originate. Observe the clouds: Heaped-up cloud indicates unstable air with the possibility of high winds and thunderstorms. Layered cloud indicates stable air and the possibility of fog on cool mornings. More weather tips are given in Section 13.

## Water conditions

If the water is very rough with many white caps, wait for conditions to improve.

## Local conditions

- Large bodies of water can be dangerous. Storms can cause large waves and there is the possibility of being blown away from shore.
- Sudden violent storms may be peculiar to a certain area.
- White water conditions may occur in rivers and canals after heavy rains and can be dangerous to small boats.
- The water flowing over dams and weirs (low head dams) is always dangerous especially after heavy rains. A boat on the upside may be carried over the top of the dam. One on the downside may be drawn too close by the water circulation and get swamped. Low-head dams are particularly dangerous because they look harmless. A boat or a swimmer caught in the current on the lower side can be trapped against the dam. On rivers canoeists know a similar rock formation as a 'keeper'.
- Early in the year, late in the year and at any time in coastal and northern areas the water is cold. If someone falls overboard there is not only the danger of drowning but also of hypothermia as described earlier in this manual.
- Tides are the vertical movements of the water brought about by the action of the sun and moon. They occur in coastal waters and may be as little as one foot or as great as 50 feet, depending on location and conditions. They generally occur twice a day and are predictable. Tide tables indicate

when they will occur and how high they will be.

- Currents are the horizontal movements of the water. They can occur in rivers, in the sea and even on lakes when there are strong winds. If caught unaware, a boat can be carried into danger. In coastal areas the speed and direction of tidal current are given in the Tide and Current Tables.
- Small vertical movements of water, called "seiches," can occur on inland lakes from high winds or atmospheric pressure changes. Height changes are usually small but can be 'tide like' raising the water level a foot or two. Seiches are unpredictable.

## Loading the boat

Do not overload a small boat. Distribute the weight evenly along and across the boat and as low as practical.

If guests are getting on board for the first time, they should be told:

- to step, not to jump, into the boat
- to step into the boat not stand on the side (gunwale)
- to step firmly and carefully as near to the centre as they can
- unless the boat is beached, not to climb in over the bow

When everyone and all the equipment, are on board, check that the boat is well trimmed. It should ride level, both fore and aft and from side to side. Luggage and gear on board must be lashed down or stored to prevent uncontrolled movement. It should be put so it will not block operation of the boat or the view of the operator.

## Inform guests

Introduce your guests to the boat. Show them where the safety equipment, fire extinguishers, flares and first aid kit are and how to use them.

Guests should be told about the proper discharge of waste, anchoring procedures, emergency radio operation, foul weather procedures, emergency boat handling and falling overboard procedures. If the operator is disabled the guest may have to run the boat. They should be shown how to put on a lifejacket and how to fasten it securely.

They should be informed about safe practices while on the water e.g., careless smoking, no drinking, sitting on the side of the boat or seat backs. When you leave a dock and especially when you approach, remind guests to keep hands, arms and legs inside the boat. Ask guests to remain on the boat until it is stopped beside the dock.

Guests should be made aware of the possibility of seasickness. Plans should be made as to what to do and who takes control of the boat if the operator is taken ill.

## File a trip plan

Before departing on a boat trip a Trip Plan should be completed and handed to a responsible person on shore. A Trip Plan describes what the boat looks like, where it is going and at what time it is

expected to arrive. It contains other information about the boat. A sample Trip Plan is included at the end of the book. To prevent unnecessary alarms and searches be sure, on returning, to close the plan with the person holding it.

## Fuel supply

Check the fuel supply before leaving the dock. Ensure that there is enough to complete the journey. Running out of fuel is the most common emergency that boaters experience. A simple rule for fuel supply is one-third out, one-third back

and one-third in reserve. More fuel is used when a boat is bucking a head wind, waves and current. If it can be arranged, go up-wind, up-current first. It is easier to get back again.

PWCs are equipped with a special type of fuel shut-off valve. When the valve is turned to the normal operating position fuel can only be used to a certain level of the tank. When the level has been reached the valve may be turned to the "reserve" setting to use the remaining fuel. The operator should then head straight to the

nearest refuelling facility. The amount of reserve varies from one PWC to another.

## Refuelling procedures

Gasoline and gasoline fumes are explosive. Take great care when refuelling. Follow the checklist below.

1. Secure the boat to the dock.
2. Switch off engine(s).
3. Make certain all persons not involved in fuelling are ashore. These days, this means everyone. Marina personnel are usually responsible for refuelling.
4. Extinguish all open flames.
5. No smoking.
6. Switch off electrical equipment.
7. Ports, hatches, and doors closed.
8. Portable tanks must be refuelled ashore.
9. Hold hose nozzle firmly against the fill pipe opening to prevent sparks from static electricity.
10. Do not overfill.
11. Wipe up all spillage.
12. Open up ports, hatches and doors; operate blower for at least four minutes immediately before every start-up.
13. Before starting engine, test for fuel vapour. Use your nose.
14. If you take portable tanks to a gas station, tanks must be removed from the vehicle before filling.

**BLOWER**

## Docking lines

At least three docking lines should be carried: A bow line to secure the bow; a stern line to secure the stern, and at least one spring line to reduce fore-and-aft movement–or to allow for changes in water level. Ensure docking lines do not fall into the water where they can be drawn into and foul the propeller.

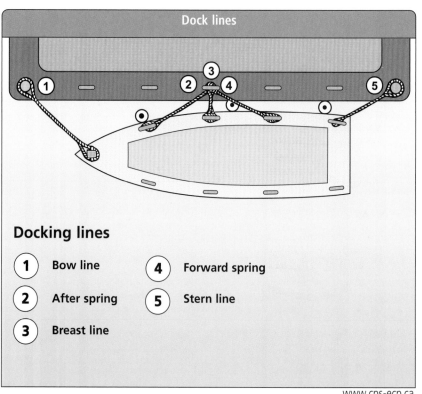

**Dock lines**

## Docking lines

1. Bow line
2. After spring
3. Breast line
4. Forward spring
5. Stern line

## Knots and hitches

### Belaying to a cleat

**Belaying to a cleat:** one round turn, a couple of figure 8's, and a hitch. It will hold forever, and come apart easily.

### Reef knot

**Reef Knot:** easy to tie; many uses; easily untied even when wet, but cannot be undone when under load.

### Bowline

**Bowline:** probably the most useful knot; easily learned.

### Clove hitch

**Clove Hitch:** a temporary knot, comes undone if there is no load on it, but can be permanent if the loose end is locked with two half-hitches.

### Round turn & two half hitches

**Round Turn and Two Half Hitches:** usually used to attach a mooring or dock line to a ring.

---

## Figure-eight knot

**Figure-eight Knot:** used as a stopper knot.

## Boat handling and manoeuvring

### Propeller-driven boats

In most power boats a water current (called the "discharge current") is forced to the rear by the action of a propeller. The reaction to this pushes the boat forward. When the engine is put into reverse gear the propeller pushes a stream of water forward and the boat moves backward. Boats with a single inboard engine have a tendency to pull to one side when going in reverse.

### Personal watercraft/jet boats

In these boats the engine drives a pump which draws water through an opening in the bottom of the boat and discharges it at high pressure through a nozzle. The nozzle can be turned for steering

purposes. For steering control you must maintain power to the pump.

### Steering

Boats that have an outboard, a stern drive or a jet drive are steered by turning the underwater part of the engine. The discharge current is directed either to port or starboard. Boats with an inboard engine need a rudder to divert the discharge current.

Although many boats have steering wheels like cars, the method of steering is quite different. Cars are steered by turning the front wheels. The front of the car turns and the back wheels follow. In boats, the stern is moved sideways to port or starboard. The bow points in the new direction. Since there is little friction between boat and water and particularly at high speed, boats tend to slide sideways when they turn. If allowance is not made for this sliding action a collision may result.

## Undocking under power

So that it does not stall at a critical moment, warm the engine before undocking.

Most manufacturers recommend shore or shallow water launching of PWCs as dock launchings or landings increase the probability of personal injury or watercraft damage.

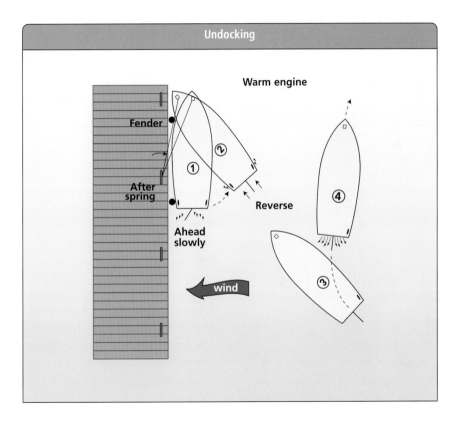

## Wind offshore

All lines are cast off and the wind blows the boat out from the dock. When clear, slowly motor away.

## Wind onshore

With the engine running and warmed push the boat clear of the dock with a paddle or boat hook. Pull it clear with the outboard in reverse. Be alert to other boats tied close behind. Be prepared to fend yourself clear of them. If the wind is strong, walk the boat to a more favourable position.

Once clear of other vessels, the lines should be stowed and the fenders lifted or removed and stored below.

The diagram shows another way of getting off a dock when wind is very strong or the boat very large. Put a fender close to the bow and drive slowly forward against an aft spring line. When the stern is out from the dock, release the line and back out. Retrieve the line and drive forward. It is important that this spring line is long enough to do the job but too short to get caught in the prop.

## Under way

When under way the boat operator is responsible for the safety of the boat, and those aboard. The responsibility lasts until the boat is secured and all passengers are safely ashore.

The operator is responsible for all activity on board the boat. A boat operator is responsible to other water users so must: control boat speed, obey wake and speed restrictions, refrain from careless, reckless or negligent operations on the water, control noise and generally, be courteous. Approximately 80% of all reported boating accidents involve operator control factors. These include: inattention, carelessness, inexperience, excessive speed, failure to maintain a proper lookout and failure to wear a PFD or lifejacket in appropriate circumstances. Operator error is to blame for the majority of night time boating accidents or fatalities. The illegal consumption of alcohol is related to over 40% of boating accidents and fatalities. Negligent operation of a boat that might endanger lives and property is illegal.

## If you drink, don't boat

One third of all boating fatalities are alcohol-related. When under the influence of alcohol, drugs or controlled substances, it is illegal to operate a boat or to permit others to do so. It is illegal for anyone to drink alcoholic beverages on a pleasure

boat when it is under way. This rule may differ in some provinces, check with local authorities. It is illegal to have opened alcoholic beverages aboard any boat that is not equipped as a residence i.e., equipped with sleeping accommodation, cooking facilities and a marine toilet. "If you drink, don't drive" applies to boats as well as to cars. Severe penalties may be levied against those who drink and drive.

## Local regulations and courtesy

Where speed limits exist they must be obeyed. In some provinces it is illegal to travel at more than 10 km/h within 30 metres of the shore. A boat must not be anchored in a narrow channel, designated swimming area or in any other place where it may create a hazard. In some areas power boats are prohibited or limited to a maximum engine power. A boat must not be operated close to designated swimming areas where other boats are moored or near fishermen. Examples of restriction signs can be found in the Transport Canada Safe Boating Guide.

A boat should not be the scene of noisy parties, a disturbance to cottage owners or shore side residences. Don't wear out your welcome. PWCs should not 'play'

hour after hour in the same part of a lake. They should move about often, especially when trying manoeuvres that cause loud and annoying noise or when several water-craft are operating at the same time. Do not modify your engine or exhaust if the result is more noise.

## Use common sense

The boat must not be overloaded. No one should be allowed to sit on the sides, seat backs, stern or bow of a boat. Keep a good look-out. Sound signals, Radar and any other means appropriate should be used to detect and avoid risk of collision. Watch for other boats, people and objects in the water, and low overhead wires.

Need to know more about Radar? Sign up for the Radar for Pleasurecraft course with CPS.

## Control litter and pollution

It is illegal to dump oil, litter and garbage overboard, on beaches, or in marshes, etc. These items must be taken ashore and put in proper containers. In some provinces, if the boat has sleeping accommodation, it must also have a marine toilet. The toilet must be of an approved type, correctly fitted and maintained, and not portable. It must be connected to a holding tank, the contents of which must be discharged at a properly equipped marina, which displays the pump-out sign.

Boat operators should remember that water pollution ruins the beauty of the area. It also harms human life, marine life and damages boating equipment. The degree and amount of garbage adrift on our waterways continues to increase. Plastic, which many species mistake as food, is a big threat to marine life. Birds are often found entangled in plastic rings, fishing line or nets. Control of the spread of invading species like zebra mussels is also the responsibility of recreational boaters. For more information contact your local Invading Species Hot Line. Untreated human waste may not be dumped overboard in any Ontario waters, or in listed waters of Manitoba and British Columbia. See Safe Boating Guide. Check local regulations for complete details.

## Know your boat

All boats have their own peculiarities. The operator should be familiar with the way the boat handles, including its turning circle, stopping distance and the size of its wake, even at slow speeds.

## Operate carefully

A boat must not be operated in a careless or negligent manner or at high speeds when others are nearby. Where no speed limit exists, set your speed with regard to visibility, traffic density, weather, current and navigational hazards. A boat has no brakes. The higher the speed, the longer the stopping distance. Operators are responsible for any injury or damage caused by their wake. This includes damage to other boats, wildlife or to the shoreline. Remember that when viewed from the boat, the wake looks smaller than it is. Be very conservative in estimating the wake you are creating. The people behind you are not waving, they are shaking their fists.

Large ships should be avoided. It is dangerous to "jump" their wake. PWCs

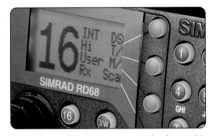

should travel in line astern with about 60 metres between them.

Because boats vary so much in speed and because you may have a boat passing you at any time, do a 'shoulder check'. Look behind you on both sides before changing direction.

## Monitor the VHF radio

If a VHF Radiotelephone is on board, it should stay tuned to the Calling Frequency (Channel 16). After making contact with another boat,a working channel must be used to talk. Since early 1999, no radio

station license has been required in Canada to carry a marine band VHF radio. If you are going boating in another country, check the rules for radio licenses before you travel. Those who operate VHF radios however, must have a RESTRICTED OPERATOR'S CERTIFICATE (MARITIME) (ROC(M)). This includes hand held VHF radios. Note that a hand-held marine VHF radio may not to be used as a "walkie-talkie" ashore.

**Remember:**

**1.** Monitor Ch 16 (emergency and calling channel).
**2.** An Operator's Certificate (ROC(M) is required for the operator.
**3.** VHF is public communication. Use but do not abuse.

Having and using a VHF radio can help both you and others. Sign up for: Maritime Radio (VHF) with CPS.

## Conserve fuel

Maintaining an efficient engine, not spilling fuel, running at an economical speed, not making large waves and adjusting the tilt of the outboard or stern drive to give best performance are all ways of saving fuel and money.

## Watch the weather

Be alert to deteriorating weather. Bad weather can spoil a pleasant day or even prevent you from returning to your normal harbour. In bad weather, reduce speed to avoid the risk of accident due to losing control of the boat in rough water.

## Know the boat's position

It is not always possible to know the boat's location exactly but the operator should always know its approximate position. In the event of a sudden storm, it is important to know where the nearest shelter can be found and the course to steer to reach it. If the operator has a chart on board, it is possible to follow the boat's progress by noting the numbers and/or letters painted on the buoys.

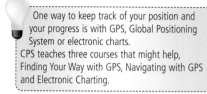

One way to keep track of your position and your progress is with GPS, Global Positioning System or electronic charts.
CPS teaches three courses that might help, Finding Your Way with GPS, Navigating with GPS and Electronic Charting.

## CHAPTER 7: Getting Under Way

From the four possible answers given below, select the one you think is most nearly correct.

**1. Dams and weirs are dangerous on:**
   A. their upstream side only
   B. their downstream side only
— C. both upstream and downstream sides
   D. neither side

**2. When stepping from the dock into a small boat, you should:**
   A. step on the side
   B. crawl in over the bow
— C. step carefully into the centre
   D. jump in quickly

**3. It is illegal to drink alcohol on board:**
   A. ever
— B. when under way
   C. unless the boat is equipped as a residence *and not underway*
   D. between sunset and sunrise

**4. Do not anchor a pleasure boat:**
   A. between sunset and sunrise
— B. where it may create a hazard
   C. unless the location is a designated anchorage
   D. between sunrise and sunset

**5. Litter should be:**
   A. tossed over the side
   B. put in a weighted bag, so that it sinks
   C. left on any vacant property
— D. taken ashore and put in a litter container

C C 00 BADCA

6. **Up-to-date weather forecasts are best obtained:**
   A. from the newspaper
   B. from radio
   C. by asking other boaters for their opinion
   D. from The Farmer's Almanac

7. **Damage caused by the boat's wake is the responsibility of:**
   A. the boat owner
   B. the boat operator
   C. the other party
   D. the owner's insurance company

8. **Before leaving on a long trip, you should complete a Trip Plan and:**
   A. mail a copy to a friend
   B. hand a copy to the skipper of another boat
   C. take it with you
   D. leave a copy with some responsible person

9. **When filling your fuel tank, an important thing to do is:**
   A. check the price
   B. take only enough fuel to get you to your destination
   C. keep the nozzle against the fill pipe opening
   D. fill portable tanks on board

10. **Most weather changes come from:**
    A. west
    B. south
    C. east
    D. north

| Answers | 4-b | 8-d |
|---------|-----|-----|
| 1-c | 5-d | 9-c |
| 2-c | 6-b | 10-a |
| 3-b | 7-b | |

# Anchoring

The anchor and the line or chain attached to it (called the "rode"), are very important pieces of equipment. An anchor can make the difference between safety and disaster. The anchor line should always be attached to the anchor and the other end of the line (bitter end) tied to the boat. Many anchors, Danforth, Bruce, Fortress, Plow, work by hooking in the bottom. They stay hooked best if a length of chain holds the shank of the anchor on bottom. A length of chain 2 or 3 metres long should be fitted between the anchor and the line.

Danforth

Mushroom

## Types of anchor

The Danforth and the Mushroom anchors are among the most popular types for small boats. They should always be stored where they can be easily reached and quickly released.

## Selecting the anchorage

Although anchoring is not as easy as it seems, a little practice will be a big help. Choose a well-protected area, preferably with a flat bottom. Approach slowly, upwind or against the current, whichever is the stronger. Check that the bitter end is indeed tied to the boat. When in position, stop the boat and lower the anchor slowly over the bow until it reaches the bottom. If anchoring overnight, allow room for the boat to swing as the wind and current

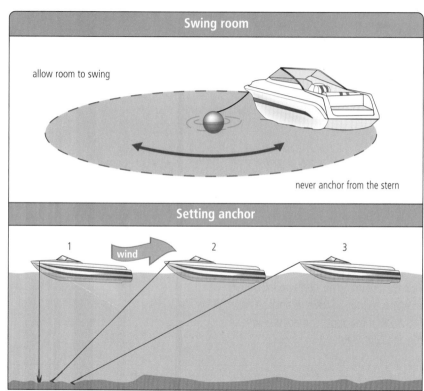

Swing room

allow room to swing

never anchor from the stern

Setting anchor

wind

1     2     3

84

may change. You need a larger anchor for overnight use and stormy weather. Lower, never throw the anchor over the side.

A small boat should never be anchored over the stern, or side, because it may be swamped by waves, or drawn under by a strong current.

## Setting the anchor

To set the anchor, run the boat slowly astern and let the anchor line run out until its length is about five to seven times the depth of the water plus the height of the bow above the water. The anchor line is then tied to a strong point on the boat's bow. As the anchor sets the bow will turn into the wind and the anchor line will stop jerking. From time to time check to see that your anchor is holding, not dragging. Use two landmarks to pinpoint your position. If anchoring at night you must display an anchor light, a white light visible all around.

*b d b b a*

### CHAPTER 8: Anchoring

From the four possible answers given below, select the one you think is most nearly correct.

1.  **When anchoring, the anchor should be:**
    A. swung around and thrown as far as possible
    B. lowered slowly over the bow
    C. dropped quickly, even if the rope is tangled
    D. lowered with the minimum possible rode

2.  **Anchoring should be done:**
    A. while travelling downwind
    B. while travelling upwind
    C. while travelling in any direction
    D. while stopped dead

3.  **When anchoring, the length of your anchor line should be:**
    A. two to three times the depth of the water
    B. five to seven times the depth of the water
    C. eight to ten times the depth of the water
    D. more than ten times the depth of the water

4.  **When anchored at night, you must display:**
    A. a flashlight illuminating the sail
    B. a white light all around
    C. a red light all around
    D. a red, green and white sector light

5.  **The bitter end of the anchor line is:**
    A. tied at the bow of the boat
    B. coiled neatly to avoid tangling
    C. tied at the stern
    D. attached to the anchor

| Answers | |
|---------|-------|
| 1-b | 4-b |
| 2-d | 5-a |
| 3-b | |

# Docking

**9**

Before approaching the dock one end of the docking lines should be secured on board, fenders hung over the side and speed reduced.

## Wind onshore

If the wind is onshore the boat is brought to a position parallel to the dock and about 1 metre off. The wind will blow the boat in. It can then be secured by bow, stern and spring lines.

## Wind offshore

When the wind is offshore approach the dock dead slow, near idle and at an angle of about 30°–45°. When the boat is close to touching let it swing parallel to the dock and give a short burst of reverse to stop the boat. The boat will stop forward motion but still have enough sideways momentum to move to the dock. With an outboard or I/O you can turn the propeller toward the dock when you give the short burst of reverse. In light winds this method works for inboards too.

With too much wind across the dock for the above method pass a spring line ashore from mid-ship or the bow. When the line has been secured put the boat in reverse and it will come into the dock. In boats with an outboard or stern drive turn the unit towards the dock and put into reverse. This will bring the stern into the dock faster. Secure the boat with the stern line.

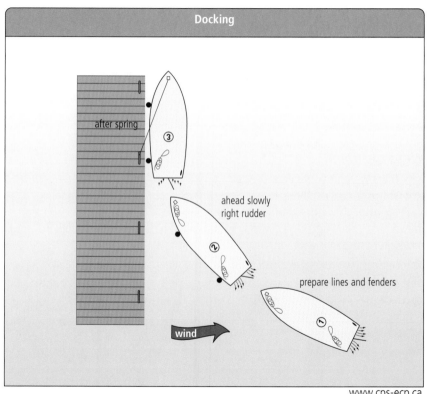

Docking

after spring

ahead slowly
right rudder

prepare lines and fenders

wind

Alternately, if the wind is offshore, the dock is approached at an angle of about 20°–30°. Pass a spring line ashore from the bow and secure it. In boats with an outboard or stern drive, the unit is turned towards the dock and put into reverse. This will bring the stern into the dock. The boat can then be secured with the stern line.

For boats with inboard engines secure the bow line as above. Use the rudder to bring the stern in as in the illustration. With the rudder turned away from the dock and the engine in forward the boat will ease toward the dock. All manoeuvres are more easily accomplished if the boat has twin engines rather than a single engine.

When driven in reverse, boats with a single inboard engine tend to pull to port or starboard, depending on whether the propeller has right-hand or left-hand rotation. You should be aware of your boat's tendencies.

*a*

## CHAPTER 9: Docking

From the four possible answers given below, select the one you think is most nearly correct.

1. **When the wind is off-shore, the best way to dock a boat is to approach the dock:**
   - **A.** stern first
   - **B.** with the engine switched off
   - **C.** at an angle of 30° to the dock
   - **D.** head on

2. **An outboard or inboard/outboard turned to port and put in reverse:**
   - **A.** pulls the stern to port
   - **B.** pulls the stern to starboard
   - **C.** stops the boat in a straight line
   - **D.** is wholly ineffective

3. **When approaching a dock in an outboard with wind offshore:**
   - **A.** cut the engine, and drift in
   - **B.** pass the stern line ashore first
   - **C.** pass a bow line ashore first
   - **D.** pass a bow spring ashore first

4. **When docking with an onshore wind:**
   - **A.** approach at cruising speed
   - **B.** swing the boat stern to the land
   - **C.** approach the dock head on
   - **D.** approach parallel to the dock

| Answers | 4-d |
|---|---|
| 1-c | |
| 2-a | |
| 3-d | |

www.cps-ecp.ca

# Locks

Where there is considerable difference in water levels between adjacent sections of a river or canal, locks are used to move boats from one level to another.

## Conventional lock

A conventional lock is a watertight chamber with a watertight gate at each end. If the valves in the lower gate are opened and those in the upper gate remain closed, the water runs out. Boats inside the lock are thereby lowered. When the valves in the lower gate are closed and those in the upper one are opened, the lock fills with water and boats are raised.

## Lift lock

This is a different type of lock in which the boats enter a chamber, like a large bathtub, which is then raised or lowered to carry the boat to a higher or lower level. Although a lift lock is mechanically different from a normal lock, the procedures to be undertaken by boaters are the same.

## Role of the lockmaster

Lockmasters and attendants are responsible for the safe passage of boats through the locks. Their instructions must be obeyed. These instructions may be conveyed by voice, lights, hand signal, or VHF radio.

### Light Signals

- A red light means that the lock cannot be entered. Boats wishing to pass through must wait at the designated

waiting area. In many cases this area is indicated by a prominent blue line painted on the wall close to the lock.
- A flashing red light means that the lock is being operated. Boats should keep clear of the lock but get ready to enter.
- A green light means the boat can enter the lock slowly and with caution.

## Role of the boater

In order to lock through quickly and safely, the boat operator must know what is expected and be prepared to do

as instructed by the lockmaster. For this reason a copy of the Canal Regulations should be carried on board. This is particularly important on busy weekends when a dozen or more boats may be locking through the same lock at the same time.

## Entering the lock

Fenders should be hung on both sides of the boat. Lines must be available at both sides of the stern and at the bow. Lockmasters generally give specific

**Loop line around lock cables**

lock wall

cable

boat line

instructions and will usually instruct large boats to enter first. The lock must be entered slowly to avoid carrying the boat's wake into the lock.

## In the lock

The tops of the lock walls are fitted with bollards, posts or rings for temporarily securing the boat. In some locks, chains or cables are hung down the walls. Lines from the boat may be passed around one or two of these. The lines will slide up or down as the boat rises or falls. In some locks on the Seaway and Sault Ste. Marie, attendants pass a pair of lines to boaters. In other locks (American locks on the Seaway) small boats put a line around

! Never tie a boat securely to a bollard or ring in the lock, because there is danger of a capsize as the water level changes.

a floating bollard that moves up or down as the lock is filled or emptied. To avoid fire or explosion all engines must be shut off, all flames must be extinguished and there must be no smoking once the boat is in the lock and secured.

## Leaving the lock

Blowers must be switched on for at least 4 minutes before restarting the engine. In many locks you will be asked to leave the blower on all the time. The lockmaster indicates the order in which boats are to leave and they must do so at low speed.

! Where there is only a short distance between locks, boats are locked through in groups, and the lockmasters notify one another. Nothing is gained by speeding between locks. It simply means a longer wait at the next lock.

**CHAPTER 10: Locks**

From the four possible answers given below, select the one you think is most nearly correct.

1. **When going into a lock:**
   A. keep to the right
   — B. follow lockmaster's instruction
   C. keep to the left
   D. stay in the centre

2. **When the gate opens:**
   A. get out as fast as you can
   B. cast off lines and start engine
   — C. wait for lockmaster's instructions
   D. dump garbage overboard

3. **A flashing light at a lock means:**
   A. the lock is closed for the night
   B. your boat is approaching too fast
   — C. the lock is being operated and will open soon
   D. the light must be kept to starboard when going upstream

4. **When in a lock:**
   A. keep the motor running
   — B. tie your boat securely to lock rings
   C. smoking is allowed
   — D. shut off the motor

Answers    4-d
1-b
2-c
3-c

# Water-related activities

Many of those who operate boats do not consider themselves "boaters," because boating is only incidental to their major activity. Every person in a boat is a boater, whether the reason is to fish, to hunt, to get to the cottage, to ride your PWC, or to just drift around on a sunny afternoon.

Boaters have a legal obligation to have on board all the equipment required for that size of boat. The Rules of the Road, cited earlier in the manual, apply. The operator carries all the responsibilities laid down by law including the regulations regarding the use of alcohol. Anyone who wishes to use a boat must first

understand the responsibilities and precautions required of a boater.

## Personal watercrafting

Unfortunately, the personal watercraft (PWC) operator has gained an unnecessary, and sometimes unwarranted, tainted image. Careless operation, persistent use in one area, collisions, riding too close to shore, and lack of good judgement have all contributed to the public's perception. As an operator, you should use your PWC responsibly, and ride smart.

Before operating a PWC, read and understand the owner's manual specific to the craft. It is the best source of information about the operating characteristics of the craft.

For steering control, power must be maintained to the pump. If the engine returns to idle or shuts off during a turn, the craft will continue in the same direction as it was moving at the point of power loss, regardless of steering device movement.

**Guidelines for the PWC Operator:**

- Wear an approved PFD at all times and preferably be a competent swimmer
- Wear personal protection such as foot covering, gloves, goggles, hat and sunscreen
- Keep hands, feet, hair, clothing, etc. away from the pump intake
- If there is a shut-off lanyard, ensure that it is attached to your wrist or PFD
- Don't operate the craft in shallow water as it may damage the unit or cause injury to the operator and bystanders from discharged debris
- Start the craft in water that is at least half a metre deep
- Upon returning to shore, shut off the engine in shallow water and push the craft ashore
- Take the first practice rides in an uncongested area
- Avoid becoming overtired as you may be unable to remount the craft after a spill
- Be alert to surroundings and presence of other boats. Check before turning and avoid erratic turns
- Stay away from water skiers, divers, swimmers, anglers and other unstable or less manoeuvrable boats

www.cps-ecp.ca

- Do not run through the shallow waters of swamps, bogs and other fish and wildlife habitats
- Adhere to speed regulations. Avoid causing unnecessary wave action. Maintain minimal speed near areas where boats are moored or docked
- Avoid continuous operation in one area and excessive noise
- Do not jump the wake of passing boats
- When used for water skiing, the PWC must be able to hold 3 people: the skier, spotter and operator
- Do not lend the craft to an inexperienced or uncertified rider
- It is illegal to operate the craft at night unless equipped with approved navigational lights
- Do not operate, or allow anyone else to operate, the craft while under the influence of alcohol or drugs
- Use courtesy and common sense at all times when on the water

"Lock it or lose it" is the best advice for PWC owners. If on a trailer, lock the PWC to it. Take off one trailer wheel, and store in the car trunk. Add a hitch lock to the trailer. If the PWC is carried in the open box of a truck, lock it to the truck. Do not leave the ignition keys in the PWC, or leave the craft unattended at the dock or beach. Chain several PWCs together. When not in use, consider removing the battery and shutting off the fuel line.

## Hunting and fishing

Unfortunately, a number of hunters and anglers drown each year, simply because they do not understand the important safety aspects of boating. They overload

their boat, stand up, do not wear PFDs, or fail to take other precautions that are required when boating. A person who stands up in a boat does not have the same balance as someone sitting down. A person who fires a gun while standing may easily lose balance and fall overboard.

## Water skiing*

*These rules also apply to barefoot skiing, wakeboarding, surfboard, water sled, tubes or any other similar objects or while engaged in high-speed towing

activities. Propeller-driven surfboards or large, remotely controlled vehicles cannot be operated in any Canadian waters (small racing models are permitted).

Only competent swimmers should water ski. They should wear approved PFDs (not a ski belt), and they should learn the correct hand signals. Personal watercraft designed to carry only two people may not tow waterskiers. Those designed to carry 3 or more people may be used for towing waterskiers, provided there is an extra seat for each person being towed.

There must be at least two people in the tow boat, with one designated to maintain visual contact with the skier. It is illegal to water ski from one hour after sunset until sunrise. Avoid swimming areas and other boats.

The tow rope should be at least 20 metres long. At start up, the towing boat should move forward slowly, until the rope is just tight. After checking that the way ahead is clear, the boat operator should apply enough power to raise the skier up on the skis.

As it is impossible for the skier to shout above the noise of the engine, the proper hand signals should be used to convey requirements to the boat operator. The boat must not be steered close to shore, other boats, or danger spots. Turns should be gentle, because tight turns may cause the skier to lose speed and sink into the water.

If a skier falls, the boat operator should circle around slowly so that the tow rope is brought within reach. If the skier wishes to get on board, the boat should be brought close alongside, and the engine shut off. It is easier, and safer, to bring a person into the boat at, or near, the stern. There is less chance of a capsize. Once the skier is safely in the boat, the skis and tow rope should be retrieved and stowed aboard.

## Hand signals

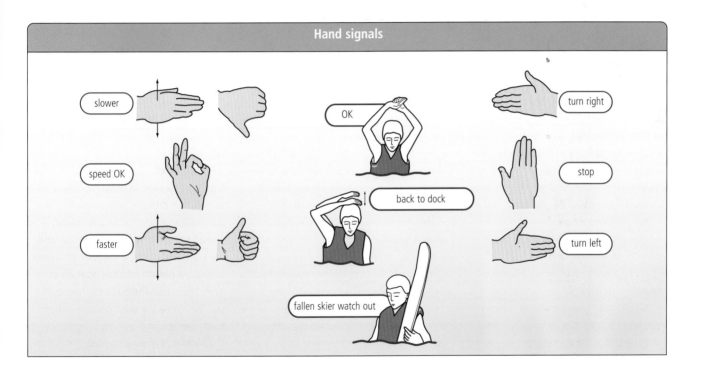

- slower
- speed OK
- faster
- OK
- back to dock
- fallen skier watch out
- turn right
- stop
- turn left

## CHAPTER 11: Water-related Activities

From the four possible answers given below, select the one you think is most nearly correct.

1. **When getting a skier back into the boat, it is best to do so:**
   - **A.** over the stern
   - **B.** over the bow
   - **C.** over the side in the middle
   - **D.** with the engine running

2. **Waterskiers give directions to the boat operator by:**
   - **A.** shouting
   - **B.** pulling on the tow rope
   - **C.** using hand signals
   - **D.** bending the body in the direction they wish to go

3. **When duck hunting from a boat:**
   - **A.** remain seated at all times
   - **B.** stand up only to aim and fire
   - **C.** stand at all times for better visibility
   - **D.** don a PFD before shooting

4. **When a boat is towing a water skier, how many persons must be on board:**
   - **A.** not more than two
   - **B.** as many as the boat will hold
   - **C.** at least two
   - **D.** the operator only

5. **Water skiing is prohibited:**
   - **A.** between sunrise and sunset
   - **B.** between half an hour after sunset and half an hour before sunrise
   - **C.** between half an hour before sunset and half an hour after sunrise
   - **D.** one hour after sunset to sunrise

| Answers | |
|---------|------|
| 1-a | 4-c |
| 2-c | 5-d |
| 3-a | |

# Preventive maintenance

Preventive maintenance should be carried out before the boating season starts and when the boat is being prepared for winter storage. In addition, routine maintenance carried out at regular intervals during the season will help avoid trouble.

To ensure that all required maintenance tasks are undertaken, a check list and schedule for the boat should be drawn up and carefully followed.

## Hull

The hull should be checked regularly for damage and leaks. If the boat is being stored for the winter, the outside should be washed with fresh water and an environmentally friendly detergent to remove tar, oil and algae. The bilge should be inspected regularly to ensure there is no fire hazard from oil and grease. Any water should be removed.

## Fiberglass hull

Check for delamination (the separation of Fiberglass layers) and for osmosis (surface blisters caused by water absorbed through the surface into the Fiberglass).

## Wooden hull

Clean, check for rot and damage, repair, sand, re-caulk and paint. A planked boat that has been allowed to dry out should be put in the water, but not used until the wood has had time to swell. If this precaution is not taken the boat may leak very badly and sink.

## Steel hull

Check for rust and damage. Repair, if necessary, then sand and paint.

## Aluminum hull

Check carefully for the appearance of white powder patches which are a sign of deterioration. Any such patches should be sanded and painted.

## Green maintenance tips

- Keep your bilge clean and do not pump oily water overboard
- Use bilge sorbents in place of detergents
- Bring garbage home and do not litter
- Use detergents sparingly and when you do use Eco rated products that contain no phosphates
- Clean up all spills immediately and properly dispose of all cleaning materials

- Use only paints approved for marine use and clean up all materials from sanding or scraping
- Report pollution when you see it to a Government of Canada pollution prevention officer. The Transport Canada Safe Boating Guide contains a list of telephone numbers

## Engine

The engine(s) should be carefully adjusted as recommended in the owner's manual. Oil and fuel levels should be maintained. Change the engine oil at the recommended intervals. Outboard motors must have the correct gas/oil mixture. The lower unit should be drained and refilled with fresh oil prior to winter storage. If this is not done, water that may have seeped in during the summer can freeze and split

the casing. Removing surplus grease and oil from the engine will reduce fire risk.

## Trailer

All nuts and bolts holding the rollers and the adjustable couplings should be checked for tightness.

Check that the safety chains are not worn or distorted and the lights are functioning properly. Tires should be inflated to the manufacturer's recommended pressure. Inspect wheel bearings prior to winter storage and repack if they have been submerged in water.

## Other equipment

All equipment, including dock lines, anchor lines, safety equipment, lifejackets and PFDs should be cleaned, checked and replaced as necessary. Sails should be checked, especially the seams.

Nuts, bolts, and hose clamps should be checked regularly for tightness. Where navigation lights are fitted, the wiring should be checked and bulbs replaced as necessary.

The battery should be kept charged, the liquid level checked and the terminals clean and tight.

## Winter storage

If a boat is stored under cover for the winter, it will keep cleaner and be less exposed to the weather. It should not be sealed up tight but should be well ventilated to prevent mildew and rot.

Small boats that are stored outside should be turned upside down so they do not fill with snow or rain and should be raised off the ground on blocks to allow for drainage.

For more information on boat maintenance take the CPS Marine Maintenance course.

### CHAPTER 12: Preventive Maintenance

From the four possible answers given below, select the one you think is most nearly correct.

1. **Routine maintenance on a small boat should be carried out:**
   A. when something breaks
   B. only once a year
   C. when the boat is to be sold
   D. at regular intervals ·

2. **Safety chains on trailers:**
   A. must be replaced each year
   B. must be replaced when worn or distorted
   C. must be replaced at the first sign of rust
   D. must never be replaced

3. **The lower unit of an outboard should be drained and refilled with fresh oil, prior to winter storage because:**
   A. old oil provides poor lubrication
   B. frozen oil never recovers
   C. any water in the oil may freeze and crack the casing
   D. the oil may be contaminated with gasoline

4. **A small runabout being stored for the winter:**
   A. may be left on the ground upright
   B. should be left on the ground inverted
   C. may be covered and sealed
   D. may be left inverted on blocks

5. **Osmosis is a problem that occurs:**
   A. on steel hulls
   B. on wooden hulls
   C. on Fiberglass hulls
   D. on aluminum hulls

| Answers | |
|---------|-----|
| 1-d | 4-d |
| 2-b | 5-c |
| 3-c | |

# Weather tips

Weather conditions greatly affect the boater from the point of view of both comfort and safety. High winds often produce high waves and it is generally uncomfortable to be out in a boat during a heavy rainfall. Operators should always keep a weather eye open.

Before starting out, make sure it will be fun, as well as safe, to depart.

- Check the local weather conditions
- Obtain the latest weather forecast for the area
- Decide whether you can handle the boat in the conditions that are expected

While boating, check to make sure if it is safe to continue your trip.

- Monitor the AM or FM radio or VHF Radio for the latest forecasts and warnings
- Watch for dark, threatening clouds that may foretell the approach of squalls or thunderstorms
- Monitor any sustained increase in wind which may produce steep waves, especially if it is blowing against a current

**After returning from your outing:**

- Ensure the boat is safely docked or anchored before leaving it. Secure the boat as though you expect a gale in your absence. It just may happen!

## Wind speed

Wind speed is very hard to judge from a moving boat.

- When going into the wind the "apparent" wind (felt by those on board) is increased by the boat's speed and appears stronger
- When going downwind the apparent wind is decreased by the boat's speed and appears to be lighter. This could give a false sense of security

The following table was produced by Atmospheric Environment Service, Environment Canada and defines wind speeds in terms of knots (kn), miles per hour (mph) and kilometres per hour (km/h). It also defines the standard expressions used in weather forecasts.

- If the water surface is relatively calm, "cats paws" on the water indicate the presence of light puffs of wind
- Patches of highly disturbed water moving rapidly across the surface may indicate "squalls" or areas of very high wind that may be associated with thunderstorms and tornadoes

Wind is affected by land around bays, estuaries and inlets. Its speed is increased in some parts and decreased in others. It tends to funnel through channels and inlets that have hills on both sides. It may blow in one direction during good weather and in the opposite direction during bad weather. When it blows across the channel, it is gusty and variable.

## Local forecasts

General weather forecasts relate to fairly large areas and are based on weather data that was collected several hours earlier.

Boat operators are in a position to make up-to-the-minute observations of the prevailing weather conditions and can often obtain local interpretations.

*Study*

| | Wind Speed | | |
|---|---|---|---|
| speed | knots | miles per hour | kilometres per hour |
| | 10 kn | 12 mph | 19 km/h |
| | 20 kn | 23 mph | 37 km/h |
| | 30 kn | 35 mph | 56 km/h |
| | 40 kn | 46 mph | 74 km/h |
| light | 10 kn or less | 12 mph or less | 19 km/h or less |
| moderate | 11–21 kn | 13–24 mph | 20–39 km/h |
| strong | 22–33 kn | 25–38 mph | 40–61 km/h |
| gale | 34–47 kn | 39–54 mph | 63–87 km/h |
| storm | 48–63 kn | 55–73 mph | 89–117 km/h |
| hurricane | 64 kn or more | 74 mph or more | 118 km/h or more |

With practice, it is possible to use current observations of wind direction, wind strength, type and extent of cloud cover and changes in barometric pressure to modify the general forecast into a short-range local forecast.

**Some general rules are:**

- If the wind is easterly or southerly and there is increasing high-level haze or cloud cover and the barometer is falling–expect rain, fog and drizzle

- If the wind becomes westerly, the sky clears and the barometer rises, expect gusty winds at first, then moderating winds and fine weather later.

- If the air seems humid, dark clouds form in the west and (possibly) there is a rumble of distant thunder, expect a thunderstorm, especially in late afternoon.

## Weather warnings

### Strong wind warning

(formerly known as Small Craft Warnings) These are included in marine forecasts if winds are expected to sustain in the range of 22 to 33 knots.

### Gale warnings

These are broadcast if winds are expected to sustain in the range of 34 to 47 knots.

### Storm warnings

These are broadcast if winds are expected to sustain in the range of 48 to 63 knots.

If you want to be able to make your own forecasts CPS's - Fundamentals of Weather and Global Weather are two courses for you.

## CHAPTER 13: Weather tips

From the four possible answers given below, select the one you think is most nearly correct.

1. **Strong wind warnings indicate wind:**
   A. less than 22 knots
   B. between 22 and 33 knots
   C. between 34 and 47 knots
   D. more than 48 knots

Answer
1-b

**Abaft:** Toward the stern.

**Abeam:** A direction at right angles to the side of the boat.

**Aboard:** On a boat.

**Afloat:** On the water.

**Aft:** At or towards the rear of the boat.

**Ahead:** In the direction of the front of the boat.

**Aid to Navigation:** A device or object external to the boat, located to assist safe navigation; it may be man-made or natural.

**All-round Light:** A navigation light on a pleasure craft showing an unbroken light over an arc of the horizon of 360°.

**Anchor:** Device designed to hold a boat in any desired position by temporarily attaching it to the bottom by means of a line or chain.

**Astern:** In the direction of the back of the boat. Also, the movement of the boat going backwards.

**Ballast:** Added weight in the boat's bottom to provide stability.

**Beam:** The width of a boat.

**Bearing:** An object's direction from a boat.

**Bilge:** The deepest part of the inside of a boat (where water and fumes may collect).

**Bollard:** A heavy post set into the edge of a wharf or pier to which the lines of a boat may be tied.

**Bow:** The front of the boat.

**Bow Line:** A docking line leading forward from a boat's bow.

**Buoy:** Floating aid to navigation.

**Capsize:** Overturn a boat.

**Cardinal Buoy:** An aid to navigation that indicates the cardinal direction of safe water.

**Cardinal Points:** The four main points of a compass: north, east, south, and west.

**Chafe:** Wearing through of a line, sail, etc., from rubbing.

**Chart:** Map of navigable waters.

**Chock:** An open metal fitting through which a line is led to a cleat.

**Cleat:** A T-shaped fitting to which lines are hitched.

**Cockpit:** Exterior sitting area in a boat.

**Compass:** Instrument for finding directions.

**Current:** Horizontal movement of water.

**Danforth Anchor:** A patented lightweight anchor characterized by long, narrow, twin flukes pivoted at one end of a long shank.

**Danger Zone:** The sector extending from dead ahead to a point 112.5 degrees aft on the right side.

**Dead Ahead:** Directly ahead.

**Deadhead:** A log or heavy timber floating nearly vertical, with little of its bulk showing above the surface.

**Deck:** Any permanent covering over a compartment.

**Dinghy:** A small, open boat.

**Discharge Current:** The water expelled by the propeller.

**Displacement Boat:** Boat meant to move through the water, not skim over it.

**Docking:** The procedure for coming alongside a wharf or jetty.

**Draft:** Minimum depth of water needed to float a boat.

**Dry Rot:** A fungus decay which causes wood to become soft and to fall apart.

**Fathom:** A unit of measure equal to 6 feet.

**Fender:** A device placed between boats, or a boat and a pier, to prevent damage to the boat.

**Flame Arrester:** A safety device fitted to a carburetor, which prevents an explosion from an exhaust backfire.

**Flare:** A signal device used to indicate distress.

**Forward:** Toward the bow; ahead.

**Freeboard:** The minimum vertical distance measured on a boat's side from the waterline to the upper edge of the boat.

**Galley:** The kitchen area of a boat.

**Give-way Vessel:** The boat which must yield in meeting, crossing, or overtaking situations.

**Ground Tackle:** Gear used for anchoring.

**Gunwale:** The upper edge of a boat's sides.

**Hatch:** An opening in a boat's deck fitted with a watertight cover.

**Head:** A marine toilet.

**Headway:** Motion through the water in a forward direction.

**Helm:** The wheel or tiller controlling a rudder or outboard motor; the place from which you steer a small boat.

**Hull:** A boat's shell.

**Hypothermia:** A serious medical condition caused by losing body heat more rapidly than the body can produce it.

**I/O:** Inboard/outdrive; stern drive.

**Impeller:** A type of precision propeller in a pump that pressurizes the water and forces it toward the back of the boat.

**Inboard Engine:** An engine mounted inside the hull, connected to the propeller by a propeller shaft.

**Jet Drive:** A drive depending on the forced discharge of water.

**Keel:** The permanently positioned, fore-and-aft backbone member of a boat's hull; underwater member to prevent sideways motion of a boat.

**Knot:** The tucks and loops in a line, used to fasten it to an object or itself. Also, a unit of speed equal to one nautical mile (1852 metres) an hour.

**Lee:** The opposite side to that from which the wind blows.

**Lee Shore:** Shoreline downwind of a boat (to be avoided).

**Leeward (to):** downwind; away from the wind.

**List:** The tilt of a boat to one side or the other.

**Lock:** A watertight chamber with a watertight gate at each end.

**Lower Unit:** The external portion of a stern drive engine or outboard engine.

**Making Way:** Making progress through the water.

**Masthead Light:** A white light on the pleasure craft's centreline, showing an arc of visibility from dead ahead to 22.5° abaft the beam on either side.

**Mayday:** The international radiotelephone distress signal for life-threatening situations.

**Mooring:** A buoy firmly anchored to the bottom, to which a boat is secured.

**Mushroom Anchor:** An anchor with a metal bowl at the end of a shank.

**Nautical Mile:** 1852 metres; 1.15 statute miles.

**Navigational Aids:** Material aboard your boat that will assist in navigating (compass, depth sounder, etc.).

**Oar:** A device used for rowing a boat.

**Operator:** Person in effective charge and control of a boat and who is responsible for the boat.

**Outboard Engine (Motor):** A detachable drive unit mounted on a boat's stern.

**Painter:** A rope that may be attached to a boat for towing or mooring.

**Personal Watercraft:** An enclosed hull, water-jet driven vessel, with a maximum length of 4 metres, with no cockpit, which is designed to be used by a maximum of three people while straddling, standing, or kneeling.

**PFD:** Personal Flotation Device.

**Planing Boat:** Boat whose hull is designed to skim on the water.

**Pleasure Craft:** A watercraft that is used exclusively for pleasure, and does not carry passengers or goods for hire.

**Port:** The left side of a boat, looking forward. Also, a harbour.

**Power Boat:** A boat propelled by mechanical means.

**Rode:** Line or chain which joins an anchor to an anchored boat.

**Rudder:** The underwater portion of the steering mechanism.

**Rules of the Road:** The marine rules for preventing collisions on the water.

**Runabout:** A small, sporty craft intended for general use, such as day cruising, water skiing, and fishing.

**Running Lights:** Proper lights to display when a boat is under way at night or in restricted visibility.

**Sailboat:** A boat propelled by wind.

**Seiche:** A standing wave in an enclosed or partially enclosed body of water.

**Sidelights:** A green light on the boat's starboard side, and a red light on the port side, showing an arc of visibility from dead ahead to 22.5° abaft the beam.

**Spring Line:** Fore and aft lines used in mooring to prevent a boat from moving forward or astern while fast to a pier.

**Stand-on Vessel:** The boat with the right of way.

**Starboard:** The right side of a boat, when looking forward.

**Steerable Nozzle:** A device for directing a stream of water to the left or right in a jet-propelled engine.

**Stern:** A boat's back end.

**Stern Drive:** A drive system consisting of an inboard engine, a vertical driveshaft outboard and a propeller.

**Sternlight:** A white light at or near the boat's stern, showing an arc of visibility from dead astern to 67.5° on either side.

**Stow:** To store items neatly and securely.

**Swamp:** To fill a boat with water.

**Throttle:** A device to control speed.

**Tidal Current:** Horizontal flow of water due to gravity of the moon and the sun.

**Tide:** Vertical movement of water due to gravity of the moon and the sun.

**Tiller:** Handle used to steer some boats.

**Transom:** The outside part of a boat's stern.

**Trim:** The fore-and-aft and side-to-side balance of a boat.

**Trip Plan:** A document that describes the route(s) and estimated time of arrival of a particular voyage. It usually includes a description of the boat, its equipment and its passengers.

**Under Way:** Boat in motion; i.e., when not moored, at anchor, or aground.

**VHF Radiotelephone:** The very high frequency radio used on boats.

**Vessel:** A general term for all craft capable of floating on water, and larger than a rowboat.

**Visual Distress Signal:** A signal used to show that you need help.

**Wake:** The disturbed column of water around and behind a moving boat which is set into motion by the passage of the boat.

**Way:** Movement of a boat through the water, such as headway, sternway, etc.

**Weighing Anchor:** Raising the anchor when preparing to get under way.

**Well:** Area at the rear of a boat where the motor may be located.

**Windward:** Toward the direction from which the wind is coming.

To learn more about safe boating courses or navigation, contact:

**ATMOSPHERIC ENVIRONMENT SERVICE**
4905 Dufferin Street
Downsview, ON M3H 5T4
www.msc-smc.ec.gc.ca

**CANADIAN COAST GUARD**
200 Kent Street
Ottawa, ON K1A 0E6
www.ccg-gcc.gc.ca

**CANADIAN GOVERNMENT PUBLISHING CENTRE**
Public Works and Services Canada
Ottawa, ON K1A 0S9
http://publications.gc.ca/helpAndInfo/hwrdr-e.htm

**CANADIAN MARINE MANUFACTURERS ASSOCIATION**
243 North Service Road West
Suite 106 Oakville, ON L6M 3E5
www.cmma.ca

**CANADIAN POWER & SAIL SQUADRONS**
26 Golden Gate Court
Toronto, ON M1P 3A5
www.cps-ecp.ca

**CANADIAN YACHTING ASSOCIATION**
53 Yonge Street
Kingston, ON K7M 6G4
www.sailing.ca

**INDUSTRY CANADA**
235 Queen Street
Ottawa, ON K1A 0H5
www.ic.gc.ca

**HYDROGRAPHIC CHART DISTRIBUTION OFFICE FISHERIES & OCEANS CANADA**
P.O. Box 8080
1675 Russell Road
Ottawa, ON K1G 3H6
www.charts.gc.ca

**ONTARIO MARINA OPERATORS ASSOCIATION**
2 Poyntz Street, Suite 49
Village Square Plaza
Penetanguishene, ON L9M 1M2
www.marinasontario.com

**TRANSPORT CANADA, OFFICE OF BOATING SAFETY**
112 Kent Street, 4th Floor,
Place de Ville,
Ottawa, ON K1A 0N5
www.tc.gc.ca/BoatingSafety/menu.htm

## TRIP PLAN

Notify the person holding this trip plan of any changes, especially late arrival times.

Name & address _____    Telephone _____

Vessel name and number _____

Vessel size and type _____    ☐ Sail  ☐ Power  ☐ PWC  ☐ Canoe/Kayak  ☐ Other

Colour:        Hull _____    Deck _____    Cabin _____

Type of engine(s) _____    Other distinguishing features _____

Flares (number) _____    Lifejackets (number) _____

Radios and channels monitored _____    ☐ HF  ☐ VHF  ☐ CB        Liferafts  ☐ skiff  ☐ dory  ☐ small boat

### TRIP DETAILS

Date _____    Time _____    Number on board _____

Leaving from _____    Going to _____

Proposed route and time of arrival _____

Returning on (date) _____    Route and time of arrival _____

Call Search and Rescue at : **RCC Halifax** 1 800 565-1582  **MRSC St. John's** 1 800 563-2444  **RCC Trenton** 1 800 267-7270
**MRSC Quebec** 1 800 463-4393  **RCC Victoria** 1 800 567-5111

## WATER INCIDENT RESEARCH ALLIANCE
### Forward Completed Reports To Fax # 1-866-221-5553

### INCIDENT REPORT FOR LAND/AIR/WATER TRANSPORTATION INCIDENTS ONLY
#### (includes on-ice and near-water)  WIRA File #:

| | | | |
|---|---|---|---|
| **Your File Number:** | **Your Tel. (        )           -** | | **WIRA Entered:** |
| **Your Name:** | | **Your Agency:** | |
| **Date DD/MM/YY        /        /** | **Time:        :** | **AM/PM** | **Light Conditions** ☐ light ☐ dark |
| **Name of specific location where incident occurred:** | | **First 3 digits of Postal Code of incident location:** | |
| a)   nearest city/town    b)   province/territory    c)   county/regional municipality    d)   name of body of water/facility | | | |

### VICTIM – if more than 4 victims, please add another sheet

| | | | |
|---|---|---|---|
| **Does the operator of the boat: hold an operator's card**    ☐ yes ☐ no ☐ unknown | | | |
| **Is the operator of the boat: experienced**    ☐ yes ☐ no ☐ unknown | | | |
| **OPERATOR**<br>**Age** | **Residential Town/City**<br><br>**& Province** | **Swimming Ability:**<br>☐ swimmer ☐ non-swimmer<br>☐ unknown | **Type of incident?** Specify from list under passenger # 3.  ☐ |
| **Gender:**<br>☐ Male ☐ Female | **PFD/Lifejacket available?**<br>**PFD Worn?**<br>**Worn Properly?** | ☐ Yes ☐ No ☐ Unknown<br>☐ Yes ☐ No ☐ Unknown<br>☐ Yes ☐ No ☐ Unknown | **Cause of fatality/injury.** Specify from list under passenger # 3, include all that apply.<br>☐☐☐  If 'Z', please specify |
| **PASSENGER #1**<br>**Age** | **Residential Town/City**<br><br>**& Province** | **Swimming Ability:**<br>☐ swimmer ☐ non-swimmer<br>☐ unknown | **Type of incident?** Specify from list under passenger # 3.  ☐ |
| **Gender:**<br>☐ Male ☐ Female | **PFD/Lifejacket available?**<br>**PFD Worn?**<br>**Worn Properly?** | ☐ Yes ☐ No ☐ Unknown<br>☐ Yes ☐ No ☐ Unknown<br>☐ Yes ☐ No ☐ Unknown | **Cause of fatality/injury.** Specify from list under passenger # 3, include all that apply.<br>☐☐☐  If 'Z', please specify |

| PASSENGER #2<br>Age | Residential Town/City<br><br>& Province | Swimming Ability:<br>☐ swimmer ☐ non-swimmer<br>☐ unknown | | | Type of incident? Specify from list under passenger # 3. ☐ |
|---|---|---|---|---|---|
| Gender:<br>☐ Male ☐ Female | PFD/Lifejacket available?<br>PFD Worn?<br>Worn Properly? | ☐ Yes<br>☐ Yes<br>☐ Yes | ☐ No<br>☐ No<br>☐ No | ☐ Unknown<br>☐ Unknown<br>☐ Unknown | Cause of fatality/injury. Specify from list under passenger # 3, include all that apply.<br>☐ ☐☐ If 'Z', please specify |
| PASSENGER #3<br>Age | Residential Town/City<br><br>& Province | Swimming Ability:<br>☐ swimmer ☐ non-swimmer<br>☐ unknown | | | Type of incident? Specify from list under passenger # 3. ☐ |
| Gender:<br>☐ Male ☐ Female | PFD/Lifejacket available?<br>PFD Worn?<br>Worn Properly? | ☐ Yes<br>☐ Yes<br>☐ Yes | ☐ No<br>☐ No<br>☐ No | ☐ Unknown<br>☐ Unknown<br>☐ Unknown | Cause of fatality/injury. Specify from list under passenger # 3, include all that apply.<br>☐ ☐☐ If 'Z', please specify |

**Type of incident (Indicate type of incident for each victim above)**

| A - rescue only | C - minor first aid only | E - major injury (long-term hospitalization) | G - presumed drown |
|---|---|---|---|
| B - self-rescue | D - minor injury (beyond first aid) | F - fatality | Z – other, specify |

**Cause of fatality or factors contributing to non-fatal incident/injury (Indicated factors for each victim above)**     M - personal

| A – drowning | C - not wearing PFD | E – | G - trauma | I - mechanical | K - capsized | N – equipment |
|---|---|---|---|---|---|---|
| B - non-swimmer | D - drugs | hypothermia<br>F – medical | H - weather | J - collision | L - environmental | Z - other, specify |

## INCIDENT DETAILS

| Transportation Type: | Length | ☐ raft | ☐ canoe/kayak, specify _____ | ☐ plane |
|---|---|---|---|---|
| ☐ power < 10 hp | _____ ft | ☐ sailboat | ☐ rowboat | ☐ vehicle |
| ☐ power ≥ 10 hp | _____ ft | ☐ PWC | ☐ snowmobile/ATV, specify | ☐ other, specify |

| Alcohol involved:<br>unknown | ☐ yes (known or suspected) ☐ no ☐ | Snow/Ice involved:☐ yes ☐ no |
|---|---|---|

   

| **Type of location (Check one answer only)** | | | | |
|---|---|---|---|---|
| ☐ lake/pond/bay | ☐ river/stream/creek/waterfall/rapids | ☐ beach | ☐ ocean | ☐ other, specify |
| **Purpose of victim's activity: (Check one answer only)** | | | | |
| ☐ recreational | ☐ occupational | ☐ daily living activity | ☐ attempted rescue | |
| **If recreational, specify activity of victim: (Check 1 or 2 answers)** | | ☐ fishing | ☐ snowmobiling | |
| ☐ pleasure powerboating/crusing/PWC | ☐ water skiing/tubing/boarding | ☐ camp/lesson | ☐ hunting | |
| ☐ sailing | ☐ canoeing/kayaking | ☐ rafting | ☐ other, specify | |
| **Weather/water:** | ☐ rough water | ☐ cold water | ☐ calm | ☐other, specify, |
| **Safety Equipment used in the rescue:** | ☐ yes | ☐ no | if yes, specify | |
| **SYNOPSIS** | | | | |

Download or fill out an online form at www.waterincident.ca.

**Canadian Power & Sail Squadrons**
1-888-CPS-BOAT | 416-293-2438
www.cps-ecp.ca

CPS • ECP

# We are passionate about safe boating

Canadian Power & Sail Squadrons provides safe boating courses in hundreds of communities across Canada. Our skilled instructors demonstrate their passion for safe boating by volunteering their time to assist friends and neighbours develop safe boating practices. Sign up with your local CPS Squadron today.

**Boating**
*–Canada's premier recreational boater's course*

**Seamanship**
*–take the next step*

**Advanced Piloting**
*–navigating beyond the horizon*

**Celestial Navigation**
*–let the sky be your guide*

**Fundamentals of Weather**
*–focusing your weather eye*

**Global Weather**
*–study the weather in all its moods*

**Distress Signalling**
*–just one flare could save your life*

**Seamanship Sail**
*–understand the theory and practise of sailing*

**Extended Cruising**
*–gain skills required to seek distant shores*

**Maritime Radio**
*–secure your lifeline today*

**Navigating with GPS**
*–get on track with your boat's GPS*

**Electronic Charting**
*–upgrade your skills from paper to pixel*

**Radar for Pleasurecraft**
*–better than 20/20 vision*

**Depth Sounders**
*–keep water under your keel*

**Finding Your Way with GPS**
*–GPS skills for use outside of boating*

**Marine Maintenance**
*–keeping your boat in Bristol condition*